The Teaching of Ethics V

Ethics in the Education of Business Managers

Charles W. Powers
David Vogel

INSTITUTE OF
SOCIETY, ETHICS AND
THE LIFE
SCIENCES THE
HASTINGS
CENTER

The Hastings Center
Institute of Society, Ethics and the Life Sciences
360 Broadway
Hastings-on-Hudson, New York 10706

Library of Congress Cataloging in Publication Data

Powers, Charles W
    Ethics in the education of business managers.
    (The Teaching of ethics ; 5)
    Bibliography: p.
    1. Engineering ethics—Study and teaching.
I. Vogel, David, 1947–   joint author. II. Title.
III. Series: Teaching of ethics ; 5
HF5387.P68   174′.4′07152   80-10099
ISBN 0-916558-10–X

Printed in the United States of America

Contents

FOREWORD

A concern for the ethical instruction and formation of students has always been a part of American higher education. Yet that concern has by no means been uniform or free of controversy. The centrality of moral philosophy in the undergraduate curriculum during the mid-nineteenth century gave way later during that century to the first signs of increasing specialization of the disciplines. By the middle of the twentieth century, instruction in ethics had, by and large, become confined almost exclusively to departments of philosophy and religion. Efforts to introduce ethics teaching in the professional schools and elsewhere in the university often met with indifference or outright hostility.

The past decade has seen a remarkable resurgence of interest in the teaching of ethics at both the undergraduate and professional school levels. Beginning in 1977, The Hastings Center, with the support of the Rockefeller Brothers Fund and the Carnegie Corporation of New York, undertook a systematic study of the teaching of ethics in American higher education. Our concern focused on the extent and quality of that teaching, and on the main possibilities and problems posed by widespread efforts to find a more central and significant role for ethics in the curriculum.

As part of that project, a number of papers, studies, and monographs were commissioned. Moreover, in an attempt to gain some degree of consensus, the authors of those studies worked together as a group for a period of two years. The study presented here represents one outcome of the project. We hope and believe it will be helpful for those concerned to advance and deepen the teaching of ethics in higher education.

Daniel Callahan   Sissela Bok
Project Co-Directors
The Hastings Center
Project on the Teaching of Ethics

About the Authors

Charles W. Powers

Charles Powers is Vice President for Public Policy at Cummins Engine Company where his responsibilities include supervision of the environmental management, government relations, corporate responsibility, and public policy analysis groups. His activities include representation of the company to domestic and foreign governments. Prior to 1975, Mr. Powers was associate professor of social ethics at Yale University and has also taught at Princeton University, Haverford College, and Christian Theological Seminary. He holds degrees from Haverford (B.A.), Union Theological Seminary (M.Div.) Oxford (Diploma in Theology) and Yale (M.Ph. and Ph.D.). He is currently co-director of the Summer Institute on Ethics in the Management of Public and Private Institutions held at Yale in 1978 and 1979. He is the author of numerous books and articles on ethics and public policy (including co-authorship of *The Ethical Investor*).

David Vogel

David Vogel is an associate professor in the School of Business Administration at the University of California, Berkeley. He received his B.A. from Queens College and his Ph.D. in political science from Princeton. He is the author of *Ethics and Profits* (with Leonard Silk) and *Lobbying the Corporation, Citizen Challenges to Business Authority*. He has served as a consultant to the Aspen Institute for Humanistic Studies and the Council of Foreign Relations.

Introduction

This essay is the result of a two-year-long inquiry into the teaching of ethics at business schools undertaken in cooperation with the Hastings Center Project on Teaching Ethics in Higher Education, supported by a grant from the Carnegie Corporation of New York.

In the first section we explore the definition of ethics and the nature of management and then try to assess the likely role of business ethics in American corporate life. We find strong evidence that the new concern about business ethics is a development in a historical trend which will continue.

In section II we discuss the history of the teaching of ethics at business schools, with particular emphasis on its close relationship to the development of the teaching of business and society over the last decade. Most business schools now offer some instruction in business ethics. At undergraduate and religious schools, this often takes the form of a separate course on business ethics. Graduate schools of business commonly include a few sessions of "ethical issues"—usually oriented around case studies of corporate abuses—in their required business and society course. In addition, four major graduate schools of management now offer elective courses on business ethics. While business ethics is still largely regarded as a "subset" of business and society, there is considerable evidence that interest in this area has significantly increased in recent years.

We do not claim that instruction in business ethics will make executives more virtuous; what we do argue in section III is that there are transmissible skills that can enhance the moral judgments of those managers who are already concerned about ethical practice. This, in turn, depends on six elements or capacities, similar to the five goals outlined in *The Teaching of Ethics in Higher Education: A Report by The Hastings Center*. These include moral imagination, moral identification and ordering, moral evaluation, the tolerating of moral ambiguity, and the ability to integrate managerial and moral competence.

In section IV we address the special problems involved in the preparation of competent business ethics teachers. We are not sanguine about the immediate prospects largely because we doubt that either the formative paradigm for business ethics teaching or appropriate education patterns for ethics teacher training have been developed. Moreover, at least some business school administrators and faculty are, in principle, reluctant to allow ethics into the business school curriculum. Nevertheless, sufficient teaching materials are available to sustain adequate ethics training, and we strongly urge that it play a more important role in the business school curriculum. We strongly believe that training in ethics can help executives think more clearly about the social and economic issues that are likely to confront them, their firm, and the business system in future years.

This report does not pretend to be definitive; rather, it is our intention to stimulate additional writing and discussion on a subject of growing importance to both business executives and educators.

I: What is Business Ethics?

A. Ethics

Ethics is concerned with actions directed to improving "the welfare of people."[1] Ethicists explore, in a wide variety of ways, the concepts and language used to direct such actions. Some are primarily concerned with the justification of this concern itself, others with the delineation or justification of principles that specify appropriate welfare-meeting conduct, and others with the relationship between these principles and the rules or character traits that guide people toward specific behavior to achieve human welfare. In essence ethics is concerned with clarifying what constitutes human welfare and the kind of conduct necessary to promote it.

A basic presupposition of all normative ethics—ethics whose purpose is actually to guide action toward human welfare—is that persons are capable of choosing one course of action rather than another and can, in fact, enter the results of those choices into the stream of human affairs. To proscribe, cajole, or persuade either oneself or others to be ethical presumes that such admonitions can be heeded and implemented. For this reason, ethicists have devoted much of their attention to the problems attendant to human freedom.

Presuming we know what *ought* to be done (and that it *can* be done), ethics must also specify who is "responsible" for doing what is required. The issues involved in specifying the agent of welfare-meeting activity are rich and complex. They are, for example, related to whether an actor caused the injury that requires welfare-improving activity or simply knows and can do something about it. They are also related to whether the role the actor is playing gives him or her the authority or legitimacy to address the issue with remedial activity.

Careful reflection suggests that we call "ethical" only those actions that combine a synthesis of these interdependent and interrelated factors. *They are actions that implement a norm which the actor is free to carry out when it is appropriate or fitting to do so.* Precisely "what" should be done to promote human welfare is related to the context of the action. The context also helps determine whether we are "free" to do what must be done. And our perception of what norms are appropriate to particular situations is intimately related to our social roles and the institutions in which they are played. These roles are usually both the *filters* through which ethical principles and concepts are strained and the *catalysts* for converting general imperatives and ideals into acts which seem doable. In a very real sense, then, normative ethics is finally the deepening of the capacity to judge accurately that "I am responsible for doing X."

Applied ethics is a species of the genus of normative ethics. It focuses the tools, concepts, and concerns of normative ethics to help specify and clarify the obligations of agents who regularly encounter ethical issues in particular sectors or spheres. Business ethics, then, is a type of applied ethics which is concerned to clarify the obligations and dilemmas of actors (managers) who make business decisions.

If the key issue for any field-applied ethics is the definition of when an agent in particular circumstances is "responsible," and what responsible conduct will consist of in those circumstances, then it is critical that we understand the role and tasks of business managers. Hence, we turn briefly to a discussion of management *per se*.

B. Management and Managers and Ethics

Peter Drucker confronts us with a fact which is both self-evident and usually forgotten: "Management is an organ of an institution; and the institution, whether a business or a public service, is an organ of society, existing to make specific contributions and to discharge specific social functions."[2] To say that management is an organ of an institution is to say that "it has no function in itself, indeed, no existence in itself. Management divorced from the institution it serves, is not management."[3]

It is imperative to note how different this statement of the nature of management is from that of other professions: physicians heal, ministers serve, nurses nourish, educators "lead out." In all these cases, the institutions within which professionals work, and on which they depend, are viewed by the professional as "instruments" of their profession.

The starting point for most applied professional ethics is inevitably the normative purpose of the profession. It is the professional purpose that provides the filter through which principles are strained. As circumstances of professional practice change, the specific *responsibilities* of the practitioner change. Some principles take on new meaning or importance; some must recede. But the *purpose* of a profession does not change, and because the purpose is itself a normative filter, the basic ethical conduit through which a profession's contribution to the "welfare of people" takes on meaning remains the same.[4]

But managers just manage ("handle") institutions. Individual managers frequently have strong personal commitments. But these commitments are not shaped by or reinforced by a set of normative personal commitments which are independent of the institutions for which managers work. It makes no sense to speak of the corporation or the hospital or the public agency as an instrument of the manager's *professional* calling. For this reason, Drucker is right—though he does not sense the full implications—when he says that we have to define management in and through its tasks. These include enabling *an institution* to succeed and to make its contribution, helping it fulfill its function by effectively utilizing its resources (human, financial, and so on), and managing its social impacts so that, as an organ of society, it enables the society to survive and meet its social and economic objectives. An individual manager, when managing, contributes to human welfare, not directly, but by way of or through the institution for which he or she works.

Powerful implications flow from these observations. First, if we are to speak of the ethics of business managers, we must understand the purposes and processes of business institutions. We must enable the manager to relate ethical obligation to his or her sphere of responsibility as it contributes to that institutional purpose. By the same token, if we are to understand that institutional purpose, we must understand both the functions the institution fulfills in the society and the constraints which society places upon it.

These general statements about management set the stage for what we believe creates a distinctly different set of conceptual problems for management ethics—and then for the ethics of business management—than are encountered in the applied ethics of other professions. The nature of management has no intrinsic normative purpose; there is no normative filter or mediating normative concept to be differentially specified. Instead, institutions *mediate* the norms and values to the manager; and conversely, personal values of managers are mediated through institutions. We suspect that much of the confusion about (let alone denial of the existence of) management ethics derives from a lack of clarity about this point.

Our argument is that both the definition of *what* norms managers are to fulfill, and the freedom they have to fulfill them, emerges from a complex set of interactions: The general norms and values that a society adopts or evolves and through which it seeks to obtain its definition of human welfare; the purposes assigned to various *types* or sectors of institutions to assure that its institutions fulfill various sectoral functions in the pursuit of those social values; the specific norms and values which evolve in *each actual institution* to help focus its particular resources and shape its own organizational life to fulfill its sectoral responsibility; the meshing of the institution's values with specific values of those persons who work and make decisions in each institution.

A graph will help diagram our interpretation of the differences between the ways in which appropriate conduct is determined in managerial as distinguished from traditional professional contexts.

Professional Ethics	*Management Ethics*
general values and norms of the society	general values and norms of the society
↓	↓
normative purpose of the profession	definition of sectoral responsibility of types of institutions
↓	↓
values of the practitioner	institution-specific values to carry out sectoral responsibilities
	↓
institutional context of professional practice	relationship between institutional values and values of managers
↓	↓
professional practice	managerial practice

C. Ethics of Business Managers and Business Management

For business managers the functional equivalent of a "professional purpose" has traditionally been the social consensus that the mechanism that controls business activity is the *market*. The general purpose of business institutions is economic performance, i.e., producing or supplying those goods and services customers want at a price they are willing to pay.

The market is an impersonal mechanism. But it is a fundamental error to think that no responsibilities flow to economic institutions and their managers from the market concept. A successful market mechanism is dependent upon a wide range of activities which allow it to control a system of economic development and distribution. Collusion in pricing and false advertising undermine the consumer's ability to choose. Misrepresentation to owners or creditors undermines the appropriate allocation of capital; the relationship between company and supplier and company and laborer depends upon fidelity to previous commitments.

The market mechanism depends, then, upon standards of managerial conduct consistent with norms of honesty, promise keeping, and loyalty *as focused* and *limited by* the market concept. These norms are not all-encompassing: most of the standards of conduct expected of seller to buyer, owner to manager, manager to employee, and so on, do not extend, at least in the same way, to competitors. In almost all cases, a promise to a competitor undermines the integrity of the marketplace and is thus contrary to the market concept.

Individual corporations have always differed in the way in which their particular institutional cultures were originally defined or evolved to achieve economic performance under the general discipline of the market. The internal dynamics in some have been characterized by cooperation; in others by fierce competition. Some have sought increased labor productivity by means of employee loyalty, others by setting strenuous production goals and maintaining high labor turnover rates. Some have tried to attract customers and establish customer identification by emphasizing quality and service; others by consistently beating the competition on price. Over time, decisions and organizational commitments on these issues and many others form an organizational ethos that further refines and specifies the firm's standards of appropriate conduct within the general requirements of the market concept.

The point is that "business ethics" is not something new. There have always been norms, freedoms, and a definition of responsibility in corporate settings. And the "market" has traditionally been the mechanism which served to tie all the activity carried on in its behalf to social values and expectations. In sum, there has long been an "applied ethics" for business.

Yet the concern about, and discussion of, business ethics, which now appears in the general and business press, arises in corporate board rooms, and constitutes an increasing part of business-school faculty discussions, seems relatively new and unprecedented. For the most part, it does *not* seem to focus on these market-based and institutional ethos-related issues. Why is that?

D. The "New Concern" about Business Ethics: Where Did It Come From?

A society, clear on its values and norms, parcels out functions to its institutions which, in turn, evolve internal values and norms to fulfill that purpose. In such a society, the norms of managerial conduct are clear, the "freedom" to carry them out is well specified, and the responsibility of managers is well defined. For example, public concern about the price-fixing scandals in the appliance industry, in the early 1950s, was not a concern about the right pricing conduct among competitors; the norms were clear. The concern was that clear ethical (and legal) standards had been violated. In such a society the "ethical dilemmas" of managers are experienced on those relatively rare occasions when a managerial problem falls "between the cracks" of a well-ordered hierarchy of responsibility.

In our view, the new concern for corporate ethics and managerial ethics is the logical culmination of a series of social transformations through which the connecting tissues that make up the "organic" connection between management, institution, and society have eroded. What constitutes "ethical custom" is evaporating. The ability of the market mechanism to carry the normative freight between corporations and society is deteriorating as the society increasingly turns to other ways to try to connect its changing values to corporate practice.

What accounts for this change? We believe that four basic factors have contributed to the erosion of this consensus about appropriate corporate and managerial practice. They are not cause and effect factors; they are interrelated, but largely independent developments. Each has had an impact on the perceived role of the market mechanism:

1. The growth in the size of all institutions, but particularly corporate ones—and a corresponding sense that the impact of corporate decisions on *both* individual lives and on political processes has increased. There is, then, a general sense that corporate America has "outgrown" the market mechanism, and

that the market was never intended to—and does not—govern many current corporate activities and decisions.

2. A growth in the scope of legal constraints and requirements on business and of governmental involvement in corporate life. These include those public policy decisions that were intended to ensure efficient markets; those dealing with corporate constituency relationships, particularly employee relationships; and those involving corporate subsidy, public purchase, and regulation of the market itself.

3. Public concern about the externalities of corporate activities that are self-evidently *not* amenable to direct market control. Air and water pollution are the most obvious examples. The confidence in the market mechanism has been dramatically reduced by growth in environmental concerns.

4. "Human dignity" and the "value of human life" are, in important ways, new priorities in the agenda of social values. The integral connection between *both* societal liberty and "distributional equity through economic growth over time" on the one hand, and the market mechanism on the other, are the direct casualties of this shift in social expectations. The power of the market mechanism was, in an essential way, premised on an acceptance of two dicta: "civil liberty is radically dependent on economic freedom" and "free enterprise means growth and economic growth assures acceptable standards of living." Not only has there emerged skepticism that growth will continue or that, even if it does, distribution by the market will be acceptable; but in addition, human dignity and the value of human life are values people won't wait for free economic processes to deliver "sometime" but want protected *now*.

A diagram will help suggest how these four factors have altered the organic relationship between corporation and society.

As these developments began to occur, they led to a series of concepts which we see as evolving inevitably toward the current concern with business ethics. At first, the concern was for corporate managers *as individuals* to try to address these concerns in the form of individual philanthropy or personal involvement. Next came corporate social responsibility, a concept which suggested that corporations had "institutional" responsibilities to respond, but which were conceived as outside the sphere of normal institutional practice (corporate philanthropy; executive-on-loan

Before	*Now*

Before

social values and
expectations, e.g., liberty/
justice
↓
the market mechanism
↓
individual corporate ethos
↓
individual-managerial values
↓
institutional practice

Now

new social values and
expectations—human dignity/
value of life
↓   ↓   ↓   ↓

direct constituency pressure

the market mechanisms

government regulations

↓   ↓   ↓

individual corporate ethos

individual managerial values

managerial practice

programs). The most recent is the concept of *corporate respon-sibility,* a notion which in no way clarified what norms the corporation should use to reconcile the competing claims being made upon it, but did acknowledge that these claims ought somehow to be integrated with a corporation's primary economic activities. In its more sophisticated forms, corporate responsibility has come to mean that the interests of the several corporate constituencies are no longer seen as constraints on corporate activity which must be managed; instead these constituencies are seen as stakeholders, groups which have legitimate interests, and at least some of whose claims should be met and reconciled in the management process. But nowhere, in our view, have there been developed adequate criteria for managerial decision by means of which a manager can "make sense" of the corporate responsibility concept in the regular managerial process.[5]

We suspect, then, that the recent rise in concern with manage-rial ethics derives less from a sudden departure by managers or institutions from well-established standards of appropriate conduct than from the fact society no longer has a consensus about how its values and practice interact to advance human welfare. There has been a breakdown in the organic relationship between soci-ety, institution, and manager upon which management has relied for its normative guidance. In this situation, other professions can "fall back on" their normative purpose and can build up again coherent, if modified, understandings of appropriate professional conduct. Management, by contrast, is discovering its radical dependence on the societal coherence on which its specifications of appropriate practice is dependent.

We should emphasize that we do not unequivocally welcome the factors which have given business ethics its new meaning. To suggest that ethics is more than what a person, who is a manager, does in private life or is more than not colluding with other marketers in an industry, is tantamount to suggesting that ethics is part of the very fabric of every managerial decision. It is seen by many as an extraordinarily dangerous suggestion. It assumes a weakening in the organic connections to which Drucker refers; it opens up the possible legitimation of conflict and uncertainty at every level—managerial conscience vs. institutional values and institutional values and practice vs. societal expectation. And finally, it opens up a serious set of social policy questions concerning the extent to which important societal decisions should be made by persons who achieved their positions through appointment processes largely divorced from democratic processes.[6]

Normative language, concepts, and reasoning set adrift from the discipline provided by a context which controls meaning and use is, we agree, explosive—and potentially subject to all forms of manipulation. For management to be forced to have to come to grips with ethics because of the social process we have described is by no means an obvious blessing. Yet to deny that the social process we have described has occurred is, alternatively, to fail to face what has become a basic reality of late twentieth-century institutional life[7] with which contemporary managers must deal.[8]

E. The "New Concern" about Ethics: A Short-lived Fall or an Enduring Phenomenon?

The seriousness with which corporations, their managers, and business schools respond to the new call for ethics—and, in fact, the very basic conception of the business ethics enterprise—depends in large part on whether the new call for "business ethics" is (1) just one more twist by which corporations try to respond to societal changes which they fundamentally cannot or are unwilling to accommodate; or (2) is likely to have an enduring place in managerial contexts and in the public mind. In our view, the answer to these questions depends on two factors: (1) Will predictable social forces tend to increase or to divert attention from the concern about business ethics? and; (2) does "ethics" offer tools and resources that can help clarify confusions, about the roles of managers and corporations; can it actually help guide real managerial decisions? (Unless ethics is able to provide guidance for, and limits to, the increased scope of managerial ethics, it is likely to engender cynicism both in the manager and the public, rather than better conduct and increased confidence in the corporation.)

In our view, the answer to the first question is quite clear since we believe that there will be five extremely powerful forces at work in the 1980s that will virtually guarantee that managerial ethics will become a central dimension of management.

1. Increasing technological, regulatory, and competitive international pressures will push corporations toward becoming larger, more integrated, and more concentrated economic units. United States corporations are increasingly competing domestically against larger foreign companies which are often well financed by their national governments. They are finding it necessary to spread research costs across a wide spectrum of products, to position themselves to bridge business cycles with products for which demand is countercyclical, and to obtain more productivity through capital intensive equipment.

But these pressures are at cross-purposes with public skepticism about large institutions. It is not incidental that in his March, 1979, testimony before the Senate Judiciary Committee, Assistant Attorney General John Shenefield chose the social impact of corporate bigness as his first argument in favor of a bill to limit or prevent corporate mergers.

> The growth of conglomerates may increase further the actual or perceived inability of individuals to have a significant effect on the decisionmaking that shapes their lives. . . individuals may conclude that their futures are being determined by remote forces. As a result they may simply lose faith in our economy and grow increasingly frustrated about their perceived powerlessness in face of very large organizations.[9]

The importance of this statement is that it simultaneously represents a new line of reasoning in Justice Department thinking about antitrust policy *and,* we suspect, touches responsive chords in a significant portion of the population. If we see government antitrust legislation in the eighties based on the premise that "bigness is bad," it will not be because of technical arguments about restraint of trade or competition or economies of scale. Instead, it will be because of public belief that remote headquarters of giant companies will not be able to hear, evaluate, and respond to local concerns and needs. The converse is true, too. If Americans decide they will accept larger economic units, it will be because of the ability of the local manager of large firms to demonstrate and articulate sensitivity to local needs in the same moral terms in which the cries of pain or calls for reform are raised. It will be because corporate headquarters achieve the advantage of integrated operations while still organizing their companies to permit sufficient autonomy to local managers so that they can exercise the appropriate discretion.

The judgment required for this kind of performance depends on the ability to integrate a multiplicity of social factors into decisions, to see these factors as real competing claims which must be resolved to the maximum possible benefit of all those who have a stake in corporate decisions. In addition, all those who act and speak for the corporation must be able to express or articulate the final decision persuasively to those who recognize the impact of these decisions on their well-being.

2. These same economic pressures are at work in the worldwide operations of most international corporations. Regional, national, and local authorities in other countries are becoming increasingly sophisticated about how their authority can be used to bend multinational activities to local purposes. A country need no longer choose between integrated production or an orderly and coherent pace of change in local mores, customs, and life patterns. Products and production procedures which find a balance, or achieve both, are becoming the *sine qua non* of participation in many foreign markets. In the future, the success of international companies will require a thorough understanding of local needs, the rate at which they can change without causing societal incoherence, and a sophisticated understanding of how these needs can be effectively related to the imperative of economic performance and efficient management.

Again, it is not just the head of the subsidiary who is going to have to be able to relate and convert corporate economics into the moral terms in which these new demands and constraints will confront him or her. He or she will have to be similarly backed by the research and engineering departments, by the facilities development programs, by the product planning and manufacturing groups. Judgments must be exercised before the plant is up, the design has been completed, the capital budgets approved. If the foreign operation is to survive, it must anticipate these issues and not just react.

3. Because of resource scarcity, industrialized societies must increasingly be prepared to make trade-offs among the strenuously competing claims of energy, environment, capital availability, and inflation. The choices society will have to make in the eighties cannot simply be "either-or" ones. They will have to be infinitely more imaginative mixes than those now being afforded, and ultimately have to be accepted as legitimate by those affected by them. The criterion of human welfare will have to be a central element in the thinking and judging process of those who develop various alternatives among which the citizenry will choose.

The public will have to be educated to the fact that there is no such thing as a riskless society, and that consumers will have to use products responsibly, for absolute safety cannot be built in at the point of manufacture without enormous increases in product cost. But if this public education is to occur, then throughout the interwoven fabric of managerial decision that finally issues in a new product, a new financial service, or a new production process, managers must weigh the societal effects of their contributions to those decisions and explore alternatives. The options they present must be in a form which helps higher management evaluate the consequences of the more basic policy decisions which locate the firm in its environment; and managers must be able to explain the alternative they advocate—either in the' marketplace or publicly—in specifically normative terms.

4. The fourth factor, which may be the most important one, begins with a public suspicion of government, and moves toward the popular call among both business people and intellectuals for deregulation. There are countless examples of simplistic and expensive rules which have emerged from governmental response to the social consensus to protect "human dignity" in corporate

decisions. But the public pressure in reaction to demonstrable social injury, which preceded the adoption of almost all regulation, has not abated. In our judgment, we will not see the disappearance of regulation in the eighties but instead see a dramatic change in its form.

Government is likely to get out of the business of specific rulemaking. Instead it will step back and set general performance standards. It will find new ways of making corporations financially liable for the injury they cause or for failing to meet more general standards. It will try to shift the burden of proof to the producer. And finally, we expect it will increasingly hold individual executives, not just the firm, accountable—and liable—for the social injury caused by corporate units for which they are responsible.[10]

Business is asking for freedom from government intervention. What it will get is an enormous increase in *discretion* with penalties attached for failing to exercise that discretion in a way that is demonstrably in the public welfare. The environment in which business operates is likely to be less, and not more, certain. Government will be saying, "You didn't like our rules; make your own. But we will hold you accountable." Business people at all levels will face, in wholly new ways, competing claims which formerly were no more than rule-book requirements. Clear normative reasoning will then become a prerequisite to sound decision.

5. The fifth factor is an extension of the general societal pattern we discussed earlier: increasing attention to the activities of corporations by the public, which has developed characteristics that will make a traditionally oriented public-relations handling of business's "publics" ineffective.

In the last twenty years, the level of American education has advanced dramatically. This better-educated and more politically conscious public is increasingly forming into single-issue groups, though it is precisely a single-issue orientation which is most inimical to the resolution of a type of question which society generally and corporations specifically must resolve.

And the way in which issues affecting businesses are being articulated is almost entirely in the moral terms of justice, fairness, human rights, and human dignity. These are basic ethical concepts, but they are also too general either to explicate or guide behavior. They are little more than evocative concepts whose meaning must be tied to particular roles, contexts, communities, or institutional relationships, in order to have any meaning. They are, in philosophical language, systematically ambiguous concepts which for both speaker and listener can as often confuse as clarify.

What these characteristics add up to is a deaf ear to a businessperson's explanation of a decision in strictly economic terms, an orientation to hear only one aspect of a problem, coincident with a general belief among an increasing number of citizens that their educational background gives them the ability to evaluate public issues. Democracy is premised on this citizen ability; and representative democracy is premised on the willingness to delegate to legitimate authority. But the citizenry does not assume that there is reason to trust the skill and judgment of business where their interests are at stake. Hence, the refusal to delegate authority—to invest business people with legitimacy.

If they are to break through these barriers, managers must learn to articulate normative statements of the problems which concern the public and propose resolutions that are backed up by an entire decision process that can be shown to have weighed moral factors competently throughout. Peter Drucker says that a businessperson's only legitimacy is performance—and he is right. But the performance standards, we believe, will increasingly be normatively defined.

Will ethics really help? We have already indicated some aspects of the qualities of management we believe society will demand in the next decade. We expect these to keep the call for "ethics" alive and well. What is less certain is that "ethical" language will serve any purposes other than rhetorical ones of critics using it to decry corporate practices or of managers using it to defend them. What we need to explore is whether normative language is capable of shedding light as well as generating heat.

The current confusion about business ethics is in large part because the market mechanism, which used to conduct the traffic between the corporate sector and the general society, no longer performs this role adequately. Hence, both business institutions and individual business people are confronted with a vast array of legal and constituent claims they can no longer merely ignore. Nevertheless, the most basic purpose of these institutions remains the pursuit of economic performance through participation in the market.

The first step toward making business ethics coherent again is to determine precisely where the norms of and duties to the market are still legitimately operative. It is important that business people do not lose sight of the fact that in many cases the market mechanism can still be an effective device to promote human welfare. Hence, the norms and virtues which foster it are worth preserving. In most cases, commitments to suppliers and creditors are as important as ever; so is the proscription against price collusion. And we believe that if the claims for it are correspondingly reduced, the corporate sector and individual managers can be persuasive in arguing that some of their responsibilities are fulfilled when these market ethics duties are met. In industries where there is real competition, pricing products at what the market will bear is responsible practice.

It is essential, nonetheless, that business managers be able to recognize the increasing range of contexts in which market ethics are inadequate. And when more is required, managers must be able to determine the appropriate norms, use their discretion, and make a fitting response. In our view, these nonmarket areas of managerial choice fall essentially into three categories: issues that involve fulfillment of a basic deontological norm (e.g., promisekeeping or lying); issues that will cause or result in undue social harm or injury; and those activities through which a corporation or one of its agents can remedy more competently than others a problem it did not cause. Whenever a managerial decision involves one of these three factors, it is appropriate it be linked quite directly to the norms of welfare-meeting activity, and that appeal to the market not "obscure" or "hide" these issues. We want briefly to set forth the types of issues which appear to us normally to fall outside of the scope of the market:

• Those areas in which governmental decision has attempted to remove certain types of business decision from the market, but has done so in vague and ambiguous statutory or regulatory language. A simple resort to market principles in the face of these ambiguities is not "appropriate."

• Corporate activities undertaken to influence public policy. This is an arena in which an increasing portion of corporate activity occurs—from efforts to obtain services, to the securing of incentives, to efforts to forestall or encourage regulation. We believe new norms are required for this kind of activity.

• Corporate activity undertaken between the jurisdictional interstices of public authority or in the zones of overlapping governmental authority. Multinational corporations increasingly confront ethical dilemmas of this type.

• The production or sales of products which cause—or whose use will cause—social injury, but which government has not yet, and perhaps never will, proscribe.

• Corporate decisions related to the cessation of business activity. When a decision is made to withdraw a corporate product from the marketplace or to terminate a corporate function (or, indeed, to close an entire corporation) a whole set of issues arise which, by definition, the market does not govern. Yet, the potential for harm to human welfare is very great.

• Corporate activities in nonmarket economies or in nonmarket sectors of a market economy. Increasingly, corporations conduct business operations in such contexts, not only overseas, but in situations where they have official or effective market monopolies (e.g., public utilities).

• Those multiple decisions *within* the corporation and its decisionmaking structure over which corporate management has considerable discretion but which are not (or not yet) covered by law. Management policy and practice related to the dignity and well-being of employees is the primary example here, e.g., equity in employee benefits and compensation; respect for employee privacy or political and religious commitments; the appropriate scope of employee participation in decisions, etc.

• A corporation's policies concerning its relations with its surrounding communities.

Virtually every ethical claim made on the corporation in recent times can be seen as fitting into one of these categories. In some areas, the scope of discretionary action is decreasing as governmental rules are extended or clarified; more often we expect the range of corporate options to increase. And in all these instances where choice remains, the canons of market ethics will be inappropriate.

The challenge of the eighties is, in our view, to help managers develop the capacities to discern that these choices are available, to help them discern which norms are applicable to their resolution, and to determine what is the appropriate ethical judgment when the choices are encountered in the managerial decision process.

It is our view that managers will most of all need to develop greater sophistication, not about the great social theory concepts of distributive justice or alternate definitions of liberty, but about the middle range concepts which will help them to relate and discipline personal commitments and societal preferences about these questions in order to shape the institutional ethos to specific managerial problems. By middle range concepts we mean those such as intervention, paternalism, the balance between authority and participation, tools for the reconciliation of or choice among competing claims, and criteria for determining responsibility when the social rules and roles are unclear.

In our admittedly limited experience, we have observed that managers who perceive that their decisions will involve ethical issues tend first to ask whether it is appropriate for them to decide the question ("Would I be imposing my moral views on others?" "Should others participate in this kind of decision?") and then attempt simply to clarify what are the several claims which are being made on them. To be sure, managers may ultimately be forced into the arena of competing moral theories (for example, whether their decision should reward meritorious performance or those who are most in need). But clarity about the middle range concepts which usher decisionmakers into the center of an ethical dilemma or help them decide to circumvent it are, in our view, the crucial ones or, at least, the chronologically prior ones.

Managers will also need to reexamine the relevance of old rules for new contexts. For example, when does exaggeration or telling part of the truth become deceptive if the "rules of the game" in a negotiation are not shared? What are the implications of the emergence of certain now widely expected individual rights for the appropriate scope of employee loyalty to an institution? When, in various crosscultural managerial contexts, does an implicit commitment become a promise?

Each of these issues becomes increasingly difficult when the

market is no longer seen as the sole mechanism relating managerial obligation to human welfare. But we are convinced that the
tools employed to see when these issues are at stake, to order the
concepts correctly, and to learn to reason with them will increasingly become integral to successful and competent management.

The manager and ethics. To this point we have focused almost
entirely on the manner in which ethical issues have arrived and
will continue to arrive at the door of corporations. But we must
also consider the ways in which the very nature of management
activity and the normal life cycle of managerial responsibilities
will make the integration of these factors in management decision
a major challenge. Management is best conceived as a positive,
affirmative, anticipatory activity taking place in the midst of
changing circumstances. Managers are constantly helping to
create or coordinate the resources at their disposal to meet these
changes and convert them into opportunities that contribute to the
performance of the firm. It is the constant *flow* of decisions that
is the most impressive characteristic of the managerial context.
Issues come to a head and pass very quickly into others. The
competent manager is one who sees the salient factor in the midst
of responding to a proposal in a negotiation, deciding whether to
follow a consultant's advice, or responding to a supervisee's
request for permission to proceed.

The competent manager must know when to slow down this
flow, when to let it proceed, when to speed it up. The ability to
consider and reorder a complex range of factors is what Whitehead has called imaginative reconstruction.[11] Others have described the managerial process as "intuitive." In any event, the
rapidity of decisions requires more than understanding, more than
decisiveness; it requires the ability to synthesize all the factors in
disciplined decisions or judgments.

If this characterization is correct, then the task of ethical
management is characterized as the capacity to see ethical factors
looming on the horizon and to deploy, rearrange, and create the
resources to reconcile the requirements of the institution with the
concerns of human welfare. It is not the leisurely process of
mulling over alternatives from a moral point of view. Consideration of these characteristics of the managerial process will have a

decisive effect both on how we define the purposes and on the process of teaching managerial ethics.

There is a second issue affecting the life cycle of the manager. Most persons planning a career in management expect to move among a variety of managerial responsibilities in a variety of locations. In fact, the ethical problems, as well as responsibilities, encountered by the manager of a sales force in Southeast Asia are quite different than those of the plant manager in a southern community, and different again from the head accountant of a subsidiary, the director of corporate compensation and benefits, the product planner, the supervisor of warranty payments, etc. Ethics training for managers must contemplate not only the diversity of contexts and problems, but face the fact that the successful manager will move quite rapidly through and among them.

The manager and the institutional culture. Ethical doctors can refuse to perform unneeded surgery or can afford patients the opportunity for informed consent to medical procedures whether or not their colleagues do so or the hospital where they practice regulates such activity. Business managers, however, are part of a web of relationships and practices which define expectations about their performance in a much more pervasive way. This web of relationships arises out of the history of the enterprise. But every manager is partially responsible for both the present and the future. The policies, control mechanisms, structures, patterns, and example a manager sets will help shape the particular functions for which he or she is responsible.

Making the institutional character more ethical is a management responsibility; operating in affirmatively ethical ways before it has changed is difficult. The conflict between the individual manager's conscience or integrity and the policies and the practices of the institution is often real. But the manager should not be viewed as a mere victim of an institution. Good managers accept those employment offers or assignments which they are capable of transforming into ones where their scruples can be maintained.

We are not unmindful of the strong socialization processes in any institution which create pressures to conform, even to unethical behavior. Our point is that, if we take seriously what we have said are the nature and role of management, it is the task of a manager to attempt to reconcile, not merely to accept, the conflict between individual integrity and managerial assignments. Managers do not belong in—and should not allow themselves to be placed in—contexts where they do not have the ability to shape—rather than be morally shipwrecked by—decisions that violate ethical standards.

What this suggests is that the ethical manager requires a sense of personal integrity. Whether or not this integrity becomes feisty and rigid or enables a manager to manage more effectively depends in part on whether there is a "fit" between the values of a particular person and his or her institution; it depends also on whether the manager has learned how to make his or her values operative in the management process. Timing, an ability to articulate arguments, and a variety of other personal skills are crucial to converting personal integrity into effective managerial integrity. We doubt that personal integrity can be "taught" in any simple sense; we similarly doubt that *managerial* integrity can be simply "taught." But we do believe that there are teachable tools, skills, and capabilities that will help in the development of managers who *understand* what an ethical decision requires in the light of personal commitments, the organizational ethos and purpose, and the societal context in which the organization lives and plays its role.

If we are correct in our description of how business ethics arises in business contexts and can help clarify the task of management in a period of rapid change in corporate institutions, then the pedagogy of business ethics is at once extremely important and extremely arduous. As one Harvard Business School faculty member recently put the point: "The subject of ethics in business has been a struggle for us since the late twenties. The fact that it hasn't flourished is a reflection in the difficulty of teaching it."[12] The first step in addressing this "difficulty" will be to review the development of this field in business curricula and then turn to the problem of teaching and research *per se*.

II: The Teaching of Ethics at Business Schools

Not surprisingly, there are striking parallels between the way ethics has evolved in the debate about the role of the corporation and how it has evolved in business school curricula. The history of the teaching of ethics at business schools is closely linked with the development of the field of business and society. Until recently, the terms "business ethics" and "corporate social responsibility" were often used interchangeably; ethical issues were considered one of among several social challenges with which future managers needed to become familiar. In order to understand the recent emergence of business ethics as a distinctive area of academic research and teaching, it is appropriate to review briefly the history of the teaching of social and political issues at business schools.

A. The Early Teaching of "Business and Society"

The belief that business education should include the teaching of the social dimensions of corporate conduct has been commonplace for at least twenty years among those responsible for shaping the focus of the business school curriculum. In the late fifties, as a response to widespread criticisms of the excessively vocational or technical training of private sector managers, both the Ford Foundation and the Carnegie Corporation commissioned major reports on business education.[13] These reports concluded that the adequate education of businessmen required that they be exposed to the factors shaping the changing legal, social, political, and intellectual environment of business. Frank Pierson suggested that undergraduate curricula in business include courses in "Political and Legal Factors in Business" and in "Business Policy and Social Policy." Focusing on graduate training, Lee Bach proposed that a two-year M.B.A. curriculum include, in its second year, a full year required course that "would try to force students to think through thoroughly *problems of business ethics* and social responsibility and their own systems of social values[14] (italics added).

Bach further emphasized the need for the manager of tomorrow to understand, and be sensitive to, "the entire economic, political and social environment in which he will live and in which his business will operate and be judged."[15] Gordon and Howell criticized the narrow orientation of business-law courses and suggested that the M.B.A. program include a required course in the "Legal, Social, and Political Environment of Business" and to help develop in students "a sharpened interest in and a sense of responsibility for the kind of society in which he will live and work."[16]

In 1962, as a response to the price-fixing scandal in the appliance industry mentioned earlier, the Department of Commerce, under the direction of its assistant secretary, William Ruder, sponsored a study on the teaching of business ethics. The focus was on the market ethics we have described. Though unpublished, it did apparently represent the first governmental report to address itself explicitly to the ethical dimensions of business behavior. The Ruder report defined ethical issues largely in terms of the personal integrity of the executive and emphasized the conflicts between corporate demands and individual values.

That same year, George Steiner, an economist at the UCLA School of Business Administration, who had been experimenting with developing a course in business and society for more than twenty years, formally proposed a one-year course in business and society to his school's Planning and Development Committee which would *"stress interrelationships between ethics and business decisions"*[17] (italics added).

In 1963, the Institute of Higher Education at Columbia University issued a report on Higher Education in Business; and in 1964, the Committee for Economic Development issued a statement entitled *Educating Tomorrow's Managers*.[18] The recommendations of both these studies essentially echoed those of the Carnegie and Ford studies. These four reports suggest the existence of an influential, but by no means dominant, liberal arts orientation within the business school community.

B. Contemporary Developments in the Teaching of Business and Society

In 1967, the business school profession itself began, for the first time, to take official cognizance of the importance of including course work on the environment of business. In accreditation standards made effective in September of 1967, the official governing body of business schools, the American Assembly of Collegiate Schools of Business, declared in AACSB Curriculum Standard IVb that the programs of its members "shall include in their course of instruction the equivalent of at least one year of work comprising the following areas: ". . .a background of the economic and legal environment as it pertains to profit and/or non-profit organizations along with considerations of the social and political influences as they affect such organizations."[19] The significance of this new standard was substantially diminished, however, by the accompanying official "interpretation," which stressed that the AACSB did not require that a separate course be taught in the area of business and society. It was left up to the individual schools to decide if the requirement would be met through a separate course or be integrated throughout the traditional curriculum.

Whatever concrete changes took place in business education following the 1967 standard were soon rendered inadequate by the pace of social change within the broader society. The second half of the sixties represent the beginning of the "contemporary" period of business-society relations—one characterized by the emergence of influential social, cultural, and political forces hostile to corporate prerogatives. Government regulation began to increase dramatically. Even more significant were the revelations of corporate misconduct and illegality that began to dominate the headlines under the rubric of "the corporate Watergate." Clearly the corporation was entering a period of social turbulence and rising public expectations with which few executives were trained to cope.[20]

Following the Watergate revelations, the level of interest in the teaching of socioethical issues rose impressively. A survey of business school deans conducted in 1974 predicted that the future business school curriculum would emphasize training in:

> useful management skills and the ability to solve the social and environmental problems facing the modern executive. Historical emphasis on skills in the functional operations of business and the ability to apply economic theory will lessen, while students will spend much more time studying such topics as the social responsibility of business, *business ethics and morals,* the role of women in management, consumerism, and problems of racial minorities[21] (italics added).

Sixty-four of the survey's 101 respondents expressed the belief that the attention given by business schools to the "social responsibility of business" was likely to increase, while 61 indicated that "business ethics and morals" would occupy an increasingly important place in the business school curriculum.[22]

The importance of exposing students to the nature of the corporation as a social as well as economic institution was reaffirmed by Earl Cheit, dean of the School of Business Administration at the University of California, Berkeley, in a paper delivered at a conference in 1975.[23] It was also emphasized in an article by William Frederick, chairman of the Governance Committee of the Social Issues in Management Division, published in 1977,[24] and in George Steiner's annual talks to the UCLA-GE Conference on Business and Its Changing Environment, the first of which took place in 1971 and the most recent in 1978.

Another indication of the growth of interest in this area since the early seventies is the sheer number of surveys, reports, and studies on management education in the business and society field. In 1972, George Steiner published an analysis of 100 course outlines in the general area of business and society.[25] In 1973, the National Association of Concerned Business School Students published a survey of 272 graduate schools of business to determine their commitment to teaching corporate social policy. A year later the NACBS published a directory, "Corporate Social Policy Courses in Graduate Business Schools and the Professors Who Teach Them."[26] In 1975, a report on the Teaching of Socioethical Issues was published at the University of Virginia.[27] In 1978, a working paper, "The Business and Society Course and Its Discontents," was published at the University of Minnesota.[28] In 1979, the AACSB and the Social Issues Management Committee of the Academy of Management published a survey of all members of AACSB to determine the status of "Public Policy/Business Environment Curriculum in AACSB Schools."[29]

C. Official Curriculum Policy

Paralleling the studies have been a number of rather important steps taken by various units of the Social Issues in Management Division of the Academy of Management—the professional association responsible for promoting the study of business and society created in 1971—as well as the AACSB. Their efforts have reflected both a dissatisfaction with the teaching of business and society as well as a serious commitment to improving it.

In 1974, a statement concerning Curriculum Standard IVb was prepared for presentation to the Standards Committee of the AACSB. It was produced by the Committee on Curriculum and Standards of the Social Issues in Management Division of the Academy of Management and was sharply critical of Standard IVb, arguing that unless the social environment was treated in a separate course—instead of being given *pro forma* attention in the courses devoted to the various functional segments of business, i.e., finance, accounting, the students would not receive an adequate understanding of the business-society relationship. Its authors wrote, "It is the entire organization that is under study, and to fractionate the study of the relationship of the organization to its environment leaves the impact of the sum of the parts significantly less than the whole."[30] They concluded: "To permit this subject to be met by being frittered away as a matter of secondary concern in other courses, no matter how well taught, is to distort the perceived significance of the subject matter in the mind of the student."[31] However, AACSB took no formal action in response to the committee report. Its only formal decision was to subsequently insert a phrase referring to "ethical considerations" in Standard IVb.

In 1976, the Governance Committee of the Social Issues in Management Division of the Academy of Management issued a position paper on the business and society curriculum. While noting the growing commitment among business school faculty to make their students "become thoroughly conversant with the changing business role in society, the ways in which business and society interface and the responsibilities of management in this setting," they criticized the extent to which the curricular changes at business schools actually were reflecting the field's officially recognized importance.[32] The committee particularly deplored the shift in status of some business-society courses from required to elective and the haphazard nature with which social responsibility cases were added to the typical policy course. The committee argued that the concerns of the business and society field required: "An integrated course of study, covering a wide range of subject matter in the business-society interface, utilizing all relevant disciplines in analysis but with a mangerial orientation, and emphasizing the whole and the interrelationships among the parts."[33]

A year later, interest in the business and society field emerged from another direction. The Government Relations Committee of the AACSB, concerned about whether the business schools' curriculum adequately reflected the growing impact of government regulation on business decisionmaking, decided to study the matter. Since the Social Issues in Management Committee of the Academy had already prepared a questionnaire dealing with the business and society field, the AACSB committee invited the Academy to cosponsor a survey to be sent to all AACSB members. That study, published in February, 1979, recommended, that "environment and public policy material be combined in a single comprehensive required course." It concluded:

> Students need exposure to this material as much as they need exposure to any other material in the business school curriculum. It is important for business students to be aware of the relationship between business and the environment

early in their careers, so that this linkage becomes part of their intellectual baggage. They need to understand the changing role of business in society to be adequately prepared for their future role in a business organization.[34]

The Buchholz report both reflected and reinforced a renewed concern with the importance of upgrading the instruction of social and political issues in the curriculum by putting them on an equal footing with the traditional subject-matter areas of business education. While observing the growing legitimacy and coherence of the "external environment" and among business school faculty and administrators, Buchholz noted that the single greatest obstacle that threatened the field's future growth was the absence of qualified faculty: few people combined a sophisticated understanding of the public policy process with a substantive knowledge of business organizations. The report recommended that a major effort be made to train faculty to teach business environment and public policy courses through an expansion of doctoral programs. It also urged the establishment of postgraduate programs for faculty who were interested in becoming skilled in this area. As a direct followup to the Buchholz report, the AACSB, under the direction of Dean Rudy Lamone of the business school of the University of Maryland (College Park), conducted three week-long workshops for business school faculty desiring to sharpen their teaching and research skills in this field during the summer of 1979. These workshops are to be repeated.

D. Survey Results

The first comprehensive survey of the teaching of socioeconomic issues was undertaken in 1972 by Thomas McMahon at the University of Virginia; it was published in 1975, and its findings were widely circulated and discussed. Of the 847 institutions offering either graduate or undergraduate programs in business administration questioned, nearly two-thirds returned McMahon's questionnaire.

McMahon found that although only 40 percent of the institutions he surveyed offered a specific course on socioethical issues, 70 percent of his respondents claimed that socioethical issues are covered in their curricula. Of those who offer a separate course, nearly one-half require it for graduation; and an additional 20 percent believe it should be required. Moreover, McMahon found that of those schools which offered a course in this area, two-fifths had done so for at least five years and seven-tenths for at least two years. McMahon concluded that "the special course of socioethical issues is not a 'fresh-air' offering that collegiate schools of business and public administration confected to accommodate the requirements of an accrediting agency or to satisfy 'contemporary' interests in the social responsibilities of institutions."[35]

Strikingly, only eight of those who responded to the questionnaire believed that a special course on socioeconomic issues was not pertinent to a business or public administration curriculum. The primary reason for the lack of more courses in the area was held to be a shortage of qualified or interested personnel: most of those schools that do not offer a specific course tend to be relatively small. But even among the smaller institutions, 15 percent reported that they planned to offer a special course by the 1975–76 academic year.

A survey conducted by the National Affiliation of Concerned Business Students a year later reported that a little more than half of the schools required their M.B.A. students to take at least one course in the social role of the corporation. Of the schools who returned the questionnaire, 18 percent reported that they had no courses on corporate social policy, 45 percent had one course and 37 percent two or more courses. Significantly, 70 percent reported that they had two or more professors with an active interest in this area.[36] A survey of 174 graduate schools of business, released in 1974, found that 60 percent required students to take at least one course in the social, political, and legal environment of business.[37] That same year, the National Affiliation of Concerned Business Students reported that more than 186 graduate business schools were offering more than 650 courses on corporate social policy.[38] In 1977, Frederick estimated between 1,000 and 2,000 business school faculty "directly teach some aspect of corporate social policy."[39]

The most recent survey, taken in 1978, revealed a significant increase in the number of graduate schools offering special courses in the area of "public policy"—a term which appears to coincide roughly with "business and society." Of the 450 schools surveyed, 382 or 84.9 percent have separate courses in this area. These courses are taught by a total of 1,130 faculty, of whom 334 work full-time in the field. Moreover, in spite of the wide diversity of approaches taken by these faculty, there does appear to have emerged a general consensus about the definition of the business and society field: it refers to "the external environment in which business operates. . . thus external focus deals with matters of central, rather than peripheral concern to management and distinguishes the field from other areas of the business school that focus more on internal aspects of corporate management."[40]

It is evident that the business and society field has become an integral and accepted part of the business school curriculum. Not only has there been a steady increase in the number of courses offered since the late sixties, but seven major business schools— Harvard, Columbia, Pittsburgh, California-Berkeley, the University of Washington, UCLA and SUNY-Buffalo—now offer doctorates in the field. The 1978 survey also reported a total of nine chairs in the area.

Yet we would also note that this field has not coalesced around any particular discipline or a common set of topics. Its subject matter is a diverse set of problems which occur in the relationship of the corporate unit with its environment. In the now largely successful struggle to legitimate this subject matter as essential to a manager's education, ethics regularly pop up as an issue of appropriate concern, but almost never as a method of analysis.

E. The Teaching of Ethics: A Resurgence of Interest

The level of interest in teaching ethics in business schools has risen strongly in recent years:

In 1978, the Center for the Study of Values at the University of Delaware received a grant from the National Endowment for the Humanities to encourage the teaching of business ethics. A major conference on the nature of corporate social responsibility was held, and the Center also developed and published a series of case studies to be used in the classroom. The final meeting of the

Committee for Education in Business Ethics adopted guidelines for an experimental course to include a discussion of various widely held ethical theories and their applications to problems in business; a description of the fundamental ethical concepts which could be used to analyze cases in business ethics; and a section of cases with philosophical analysis.[41]

The Society for Values in Higher Education, in conjunction with the School of Organization and Management (SOM) at Yale, has completed a two-year project that examined the types of pedagogy most appropriate to managerial ethics training. Its co-directors have been Charles Powers and SOM Associate Dean, Douglas Yates. This project, the Institute on Ethical Issues in the Management of Public and Private Institutions, conducts two-week summer seminars for both practitioners and academics in which several pedagogical styles are being tested. To date, there are about 75 academic alumni of this program, most of whom are developing courses at the professional school or undergraduate level in 52 colleges and universities. About 15 management schools have been represented. Curricular materials from a summary of this unique experiment are anticipated in early 1980 and the Society is planning a seminar for mid-career managers for the summer of 1980.[42]

A Center for Business Ethics has been created at Bentley College under the direction of Michael Hoffman. The Center has had two conferences dealing with various aspects of the relationship between business and society and has published and disseminated a collection of business ethics course syllabi and a bibliography. It plans to hold conferences on business ethics annually, featuring both academic and business participants.[43]

The Colgate Darden Graduate School of Business Administration at the University of Virginia, in addition to sponsoring the survey referred to earlier, also published, in 1977, a book-length "Bibliography of Business Ethics, 1971–75."[44]

In 1979, three textbooks in the area of business ethics were published: *Ethical Issues in Business: A Philosophical Approach*, edited by Thomas Donaldson and Patricia H. Werhane; *Ethical Theory and Business*, edited by Tom L. Beauchamp and Norman

THE TEACHING OF ETHICS AT BUSINESS SCHOOLS   33

E. Bowie; and *Moral Issues in Business* edited by Vincent Barry.[45]

For the last three years at Harvard University, Professor Preston Williams of the Divinity School and John Matthews of the Graduate School of Business Administration have been teaching a joint course on business ethics open to students from both schools. The first half of the course consists of readings from various ethics texts; the second half seeks to apply these principles to specific case studies involving business decisions.

A somewhat similar course, taught by Jon P. Gunnemann, has been offered for several years at Yale's School of Organization and Management; one difference is that it includes both a historical component and a social-ethical critique of the consequences of market systems as currently organized.

Professor Larue Tone Hosmer has prepared a series of case studies on personal ethics in business organizations, based primarily on the reported experiences of recent graduates in the M.B.S. program of the University of Michigan. In each case, graduates of the school were asked to make an immediate decision that had very apparent moral and economic consequences. Hosmer received a teaching innovation award from Exxon for his efforts.

In the spring of 1979, Kirk Hansen, hired, in part, to upgrade the teaching of ethics at the Graduate School of Business at Stanford, and Larue Tone Hosmer, as visiting professor, jointly taught an experimental course in business ethics.

During the spring of 1980, the School of Business Administration and the School of Law at the University of California at Berkeley are offering a joint course in business and legal ethics; the experimental course will emphasize ethical issues common to both professions.

In his annual report to the Harvard University community, President Derek Bok criticized the Harvard Business School for failing to adequately educate future executives about the role of the corporation in society. Among the specific issues that he argued needed more attention from business school faculty was the "problem of ethics and the study of appropriate means that businessmen can employ to achieve their goals." Bok especially raised the following ethical issues as in need of further academic inquiry:

"How can companies reconcile the loyalty they expect from their employees with the right to dissent and speak out? At what point do efforts to motivate workers become transformed into unreasonable forms of manipulation? Can firms be expected to refrain from bribery and deceit in markets where their competitors regularly engage in such tactics? What can chief executives do to set demanding goals for their subordinates without inducing them to fix prices or otherwise violate the law?"[46]

The business community is beginning to make funds available for the teaching of ethics at business schools. The University of Santa Clara received monies from several major corporations, most with headquarters on the West Coast, to establish a chair in business ethics. The chair will be occupied on a rotating basis. The Walter and Evelyn Haas Jr. Fund has made a substantial grant to the business schools at the University of California at Berkeley and Stanford in order to encourage the integration of ethical concerns into their curriculum and to promote the discussion of ethical issues in both the university and business communities. The two schools are jointly sponsoring a national workshop on the teaching of ethics to M.B.A. students during the spring of 1980. In addition, two companies, Allied Chemical and Cummins Engine, now include seminars on ethical issues in their own management training programs.

F. How Ethics Are Taught

At present, courses dealing with socioethical issues fall into three broad categories. The first emphasizes the interaction of government controls over business, and the ways in which corporations are seeking to "respond" to increasing government regulation. Reflecting the view that the scope of corporate discretion is narrowing as a result of increased governmental controls over business, this perspective seeks to provide managers with an understanding of the new regulatory environment. In effect, it reduces the corporation's relationship to "society" to its relationship with "government."

This approach does seem capable of resolving a troublesome problem, namely, the absence of an underlying theory: corporate social policy becomes in effect a subset of the study of public policy. To the extent that this approach becomes influential, there is likely to be a convergence of perspectives between schools of public policy (or public administration) and business schools. This approach, however, explicitly avoids the discussion of values or moral issues. Its standards for judging the impact of public policies on business tend to be rigidly economic, and assume a future for the corporate manager quite different from the one we forecast in section I. Instead, it appears to be oriented toward helping managers defend themselves from a hostile political environment.

A second orientation specifically emphasizes the ethical dimensions of corporate conduct. There has been a striking increase recently in the number of courses informed by an explicitly religious or philosophical orientation. These courses tend to focus exclusively on "business ethics." For the most part, they are taught, either wholly or in part, by faculty trained in either religion or philosophy, and tend to emphasize case studies and articles that make explicit reference to the morality of individual decisions made by executives. In sharp contrast to courses in the first category, many include readings that advance specific ethical principles—either secular or religious—and then seek to apply them to the world of business. They also stress the use of various games that encourage students to formulate and clarify the ethical assumptions that underlie their personal belief systems. These courses play a particularly important role at business schools located in religious institutions, as well as at several undergraduate schools of business, where they often substitute for business and society courses.

Courses in "business ethics" have also been introduced into a few of the major M.B.A. programs. In addition to the courses already established at Harvard and Yale, both Stanford and the University of California at Berkeley are offering business ethics courses for credit during the 1979–80 academic year. These courses supplement course offerings in business and society; without exception they are electives and have been generally offered as a response to the particular interests of students and faculty.

In a third orientation, ethics is not taught as a separate course; instead it is integrated into either a business and society course or a course in business policy. This is the most common way in which ethics is taught in the business school curriculum. These courses are most frequently taught by faculty trained in management, though several are taught by economics, law, or political science faculty. Most of these courses cover a broad range of topics and problems, including business-government relations, social responsibility, and specific areas of corporate social performance such as consumerism, ecology, antitrust, energy, and corporate governance. Many include background material on the principles of capitalism and the history of business in America.

While many of these courses address themselves to "ethics and values" they do so without any discernible normative orientation, such as we have outlined. Ethics is largely treated as another problem with which management must learn to cope or as an issue about which there is now considerable controversy. A handful of issues are defined as ethical ones. But most public issues that affect either the corporation or the public policy process are analyzed chiefly in terms of their impact on management or the society.

In sum, the vast majority of business schools do include some discussion of ethical issues within the curriculum; only a minority discuss the external environment of business without any reference to ethical concerns. On the other hand, relatively few business schools offer courses that orient the consideration of economic and management decisions by using ethical concepts and topics as criteria for choice. An increase in the number of business school courses with ethics in their title should not be confused with an increase in teaching business ethics; many of these courses are essentially standard business and society courses which devote a few sessions to ethical concerns. Although the subject matter of most business and society courses does overlap with business ethics, there remains an important difference in perspectives; most of the issues presented in business and society courses tend to be examined in terms of social, political, economic, management, or historical categories—not ethical ones. To the extent that an ethical perspective is emphasized in most business school curriculums, it is as a relatively small part of either the business and society or business policy courses.

In our view, both the relatively low volume of ethics teaching and the uncertainty about its proper locus, content, and methods result from the fact that teachers are generally not yet clear about the pedagogical implications of the array of issues we have discussed earlier. It is to those issues that we now turn.

III: Goals, Methods, and Contexts of Business Ethics Teaching

This review of business school efforts to incorporate ethics into management training has convinced us that business schools are not generally conceiving of ethics as a discipline capable of helping to guide managerial decision. Even Derek Bok, whose recent advocacy in behalf of business ethics has stirred considerable controversy, seems to suggest that ethics has a limited role. He defines pedagogy in business ethics as "the study of the appropriate means that businessmen can employ to achieve their goals."[47] This suggests that ethics is seen as a constraint on action to achieve predefined purposes. Our view, as delineated in section I, is that ethics may well help managers actively to sort out the ends as well.

For us, the pedagogical task is to help managers, or managers-to-be, to learn: (1) How to clarify, relate, and deal with tensions between their own commitments and those that are implicit in the corporations for which they work or in specific tasks they are assigned. This relationship, in turn, depends on learning (2) how to clarify the relationship between the ethos or culture of a given corporation and the proper scope of "market ethics" as it arises in the context of actual managerial decision. This relationship, in turn, requires clarification of (3) how "market ethics" are related to the new expectations of corporations arising out of the changing character of the corporate role in society and the changing nature of social values. Again, managers must have criteria for knowing when these expectations are legitimate and how to choose among them when they conflict.

The goal of business ethics training is not, then, to teach the manager how to resolve a specific moral dilemma. Such a purpose entirely misconceives the nature of the management task. The goal is to develop the *capabilities* to put managerial situations under ethical discipline. When so conceived, what business ethics training seeks is to develop the faculty of, or capacities for, moral judgment in business contexts: the ability to integrate a concern for the welfare of people with one's managerial role and to implement that concern competently.

We have used the phrase, "develop the faculty for moral judgment," for a reason. This is not a faculty which is "created" or in any simple sense "imparted." We are mindful of the warning that Kant gave about the relationship between understanding and judgment: "[T]hough understanding is capable of being instructed, and of being equipped with rules, judgment is a peculiar talent which can be practiced only, and cannot be taught. . . . In the absence of such a natural gift no rule that may be prescribed to him for this purpose can ensure against misuse."[48]

While the warning will inform much of what we suggest about the style, context, and content of business ethics teaching, it does not lead us to the conclusion that training in business ethics is impossible. We believe that there are six elements or capacities on which moral judgment in management depends:[49]

A. Elements of Moral Judgment

1. Moral Imagination

The ability to perceive that a web of competing economic claims is, simultaneously, a web of moral relationships. A person with moral imagination is not only sensitive to, but hunts out the hidden dimensions of where people are likely to get hurt; a person who anticipates being thrust into situations where the managerial choice will be intolerable and imagines how the events leading to such a choice could be avoided.

Because the business person can argue that his or her actions are under the stern discipline of both market and government control, it is tempting for the manager to rationalize away his or her ability to make morally self-conscious choices. Managers do not, for a variety of reasons, desire the changes we have described in section I. And many of the moral factors attendant— and consequent—to business decisions are remote and distant from the decisionmaker. These factors cohere to help reinforce a natural human inclination to which J. K. Galbraith has pointed, that "the privilege of controlling the actions or affecting the income and property of other persons is something that none of us profess to seek or admit possessing."[50] Managers will frequently go to great lengths to persuade themselves and others that they do not possess it.

In addition, because managers live in a world where quantifiable performance is both the central motivation and the primary method of evaluation,[51] the more amorphous character of moral issues may make them seem unimportant.

Stimulating the moral imagination, then, may well be the most difficult element of moral judgment to evoke. If this goal is not met, the other elements of moral judgment are irrelevant because the "space" needed for its employment will not have been opened.

2. Moral identification and Ordering

This is the ability to see which of the moral claims being made are relevant or irrelevant, clearly distinguished or chaotically asserted; to determine whether the moral language that is being introduced by others is merely rhetorical or accurately states a real moral problem. It is also the ability to see behind the seemingly "merely descriptive" or amoral language in which managerial problems are typically described to the issues where human welfare is importantly at stake. In sum, we are describing a capacity to control the moral factors of a managerial situation so that confusion is minimal and a situation is created in which effective decision is possible. Put another way, we are describing the ability to order moral factors much as the manager orders the economic factors in preparation for a decision. Hence, we are describing a process similar to normal managerial reasoning which locates risk and probable benefit and links both risk and benefit to available resources.

But managers who possesses managerial judgment must be able to take these steps quickly, an ability which grows only through repetition. Since business decisions are always part of an ongoing process, most recognition and ordering of ethical issues must be done in the course of regular activity.

In our experience, the successful or unsuccessful resolution of the most important moral problems is determined by the immediate response of the manager after the moral issue is raised. Business *analysts* are capable of using their finance training to "run the numbers"; but *managers* must develop the capacity to leap through these same processes—and be right within one or two percentage points—as they calculate the benefits of one plant location over another, the consequences of a novel way of giving a discount, and so on, and then judge whether their calculations are close enough to "close the deal" or take the risk of losing it while waiting to complete the analysis. So also for ethics. The skills of moral identification must be honed so well and repeated so often so that they are available when the issue arises.

Accordingly, the capacity to recognize ethical issues as issues which can be addressed rationally, and not merely as involving inchoate emotional responses, is an important element of business ethics teaching. But it is a difficult capacity to develop. What is needed is the ability quickly to locate the nub of the moral problem and to assure that the right categories are being employed. For example, extortion and the fear of possible bodily harm raise significantly different ethical issues than do active efforts to bribe. If the issue is not correctly identified, ethical reasoning about it is awry from the start.

3. Moral Evaluation

Once the moral environment of a decision is recognized and ordered and the "nub" of the issue becomes clear, then the alternatives can be weighed and reasoning about them can begin. In our view, the analytical ethical *skills* required for business decisions do not, in and of themselves, differ dramatically from those needed for ethical analysis in other contexts. Indeed, the minimal skills of coherence and consistency needed for normative reasoning are highly prized in business contexts. And business people become extremely agile in "practical reasoning" in the nonmoral sense of that term. If managers can be convinced of the importance of clear definition of principles, patterns of ethical justification, and the need to judge probable consequences in moral terms, they can develop unusual facility in such analyses. It does not, for example, take business persons long to see the necessity for moving to other criteria when a "bundle of rights" call for incompatible actions—*if* they can be convinced both that the incompatibility is not proof of the mere relativity of moral matters and that the search for such higher principles can actually help inform decisions.

On the other hand, we have consistently argued here that the real difficulty in evaluating moral dilemmas is that specific institutional goals and purposes must also be incorporated in managerial decisions. The capacity for moral analysis that we have in mind will not permit a chronological ordering—first, "what is ethical?" and then, "what is institutionally possible?" Rather, we are seeking an evaluation that relates the protection of human welfare to the ongoing process of meeting or reforming institutional purposes, as a way of helping a manger to be a responsible agent of his or her firm.

The teaching of analytical skills will, then, fail—more quickly with managers than with most—if the teacher cannot demonstrate that rigorous analysis both leads somewhere and can be made to pay off in more morally adequate decisions. We suggest that the ethics teacher's frequent response, "That raises even more complex and abstract questions," may be the most debilitating pedagogical ploy for the teaching of managers. It may "work" with intellectually enthusiastic professional school students; real managers will insist on the tools which will yield an *answer,* which can be both justified and "works"; their world is one of real—not hypothetical—decisions with real, live consequences.

4. Tolerating Moral Disagreement and Ambiguity

Observers want answers because they want closure; managers, because they really need them. And when managers cite ethical disagreement and ambiguity, it is usually part of an argument for forgetting ethics altogether. But both disagreement and ambiguity are real in ethics. Hence, we see the development of this capacity less as a final than as a proximate goal—the challenging ped-

agogical task of "opening up" the space so that ethics has room
and a place in business decisions, while honestly acknowledging
that the justifications for moral matters are not ultimately as
"coercive" as mathematics and may, in fact, finally rest on
"decision."[52] Pedagogically, it is probably less useful to preach
that people should tolerate direct disagreement and ambiguity
than to attempt to engage managers in the process of understanding how and why disagreement and ambiguity arise. The point is
that "seeking the welfare of others" involves sensitive attention
to the moral view of others. In fast-moving managerial processes
it is easy to forget that a corporate decision can affect thousands
of people. We suggest that in business ethics development of the
capacity to understand the diverse commitments of those whom
managers affect is the direct goal, of which the ability to tolerate
disagreement and ambiguity is an important corollary.

These four elements are the capacities needed for making
moral *judgments,* and their development is the primary goal of
business ethics teaching. But mature managerial *judgment* is more
than the making of judgments. Two more capacities need development.

5. Integrating Managerial Competence and Moral Competence

For the manager the ability to make an ethical decision is of no
value, if it is not linked to managerial competence, the ability to
create and coordinate the resources for which one is responsible,
to shape the context in which managerial decisions must be
made, rather than merely be shaped by them. One way to explain
the implications of this for the ethics of management is to distinguish between two kinds of ethics: the "ethics of the head in the
hands" as compared to the "ethics of anticipation." Ethical issues
in business are typically thought to arise in unusual situations in
which the manager is faced with an intolerable choice between,
for example, commitments to employees and the demands of
customers, or between the preservation of community health and
the need for a good fourth quarter to maintain investor confidence. The manager then is pictured leaning back with hands
over wincing face, abstracted from the normal process of decisionmaking and wrestling with personal conscience. Every ethical
manager will face moments like this, but the ethics about which
we have been talking are not typically of this sort.

Instead, they are better characterized as management in which every evolving decision is, from one perspective, a moral one, anticipating that tomorrow or next week there will be a claim coming from one or another constituency or stakeholder and thus requiring skilled efforts to assure that, when it arrives, the resources are there to respond. The manager should be good at forecasting how such concerns should be dealt with, how they can all be maximized, or why they can only be partly met. He or she should be able to decide when the ethical issue should be raised, to lead others through the process of implementing the decision, and explaining why the chosen response is justified and not a mere rationalization.

Some of these capacities are, quite evidently, not ones for which an ethics course is the most important learning context. Others, such as practice in articulating moral decisions to diverse constituencies, should be goals of ethics teaching. Sound moral judgment for managers involves much more than the capacity to make an ethical decision; it involves converting decision into institutional operations.

6. A Sense of Moral Obligation

Behind all of the other capacities, as both the motivator and guide, must be a manager's sense of moral obligation and integrity which drives the process, holds a person on course, and creates a feeling of moral responsibility wherever the manager has discretion and knows that human welfare is at stake. We view this as the element of moral judgment over which the teacher has the least direct influence. The absence of this sense in a student cannot be corrected. But it is within the purview of good pedagogy to ensure that for those students who have this sense the teaching process helps demonstrate its relevance to the managerial context.

B. Levels and Contexts of Business Ethics Teaching

We believe the development of these six elements of moral judgment in management should be a goal in every context in which business ethics is taught. But the crucial issue in determining how they are taught is what the "student" brings to the classroom. This issue should, we believe, shape both content and pedagogical style for the several contexts in which business ethics teaching occurs. Two of the major philosohical minds in the Western tradition, Kant and Whitehead, have drawn our attention to closely related aspects of this issue: The relationship between understanding and judgment and the relationship between imagination and experience.

1. Understanding and Judgment

We have already noted Kant's view that judgment is a faculty which can be developed only. But he clearly believes that understanding—the ability to learn the rules—is something that can be imparted: "as it were, grafted upon a limited understanding."[53] The capacities we have discussed require the ability to clarify concepts, to reason clearly, etc., skills which can be sharpened in abstraction from real application. But when it comes to the application of these skills, Kant makes a suggestion which, in our view, helps uncloud the long-standing business school debate about the priority to be given to analytic as distinguished from case-based teaching:

> [S]harpening of judgment is indeed the one great benefit of examples. Correctness and precision of intellectual insight, on the other hand, they more usually somewhat impair. For only very seldom do they adequately fulfill the requirements of the rule. . . . Besides, they often weaken that effort which is required of the understanding to comprehend properly the rules in their universality, in independence of the particular circumstance of experience, and so accustom us to use rules rather as formulas than as principles. . . . Examples are thus the go-cart of the judgment; and those who are lacking in the natural talent can never dispense with them.[54]

The inference we draw is that understanding is the needed precursor to judgment. Textbook teaching may be most appropriate for it; but when the student stands close to and is being prepared to make judgments about managerial situations, case material is the most appropriate pedagogical resource.

2. Imagination and Experience

Whitehead, in a lecture inaugurating the new campus of the

Harvard Business School in 1929, provided what we believe is an insight complementary to Kant's:

> Imagination is not to be divorced from the facts: it is a way of illuminating the facts....The tragedy of the world is that those who are imaginative have but slight experience, and those who are experienced have feeble imaginations. . . . The way in which a university should function in the preparation for an intellectual career, such as modern business or one of the older professions, is by promoting the imaginative consideration of the various general principles underlying that career. Its students thus pass into their period of technical apprenticeship with their imaginations already practiced in connecting details with general principles. The routine then receives its meaning, and also illuminates the principles which give it that meaning. Hence, instead of a drudgery issuing in a blind rule of thumb, the properly trained man has some hope of obtaining an imagination disciplined by detailed facts and by necessary habits.[55]

If Whitehead is right, then the task of business ethics teaching of persons preparing for managerial careers is quite different from that of those already immersed in them. And when combined with Kant's analysis, Whitehead suggests to us a schema for the teaching of business ethics to persons at different career stages. The chart which follows is, probably, overspecific, but does, we think, generally suggest the appropriate emphasis which should be given to the several elements of moral judgment at the various levels of managerial experience.

C. Undergraduate Curricula

Business ethics courses are springing up in many undergraduate schools as part of humanities programs.[56] We have severe doubts about the value of these programs, if they are conceived as "preparatory" courses for business careers. The two essential ingredients for making business ethics material come alive and be real are absent in undergraduates: (1) experience with dilemmas and the restraints on responsible action encountered in business contexts; and (2) usually, a clear and unambiguous career commitment to take on the role of manager in a business institution.

Emphases in Business Ethical Teaching:

	Undergraduate	Professional Education	Continuing Education for Practitioners	Education for Top Management
Moral Imagination:				
general	A			
business contexts		A	A	
Identification and Ordering of Moral Issues:				
general	A			
business contexts		A	A	A
Moral Analysis:				
general	A			
business contexts		A	A	A
Tolerating Disagreement:	B	B	B	B
Integration of Managerial and Moral Competence:			A	A
Creating a Sense of Moral Obligation:	B	B		

A - Most Important
B - Very Important

In the remainder of this section we will address the several levels and contexts in which business ethics is being, and can be, taught in an effort to elucidate the implications of this chart.

For those students who will be heading for business careers, beginning with an undergraduate course in business ethics is akin to beginning with business or labor economics prior to Economics 101. However, an undergraduate course in the principles, procedures, and history of ethics and for the nature of "practical reasoning" is important. How can one later wrestle with the proper scope of, and constraints on, worker participation in cor-porate life without either production experience *or* knowing something about Berlin's "Two Concepts of Liberty," Mill's *On Liberty,* and the varieties of ways in which the right of self-determination have been understood in the history of ethical and political thought? Undergraduate curricula do not provide produc-tion experience, but can provide Mill. In many undergraduate ethics courses examples from business can be used to illuminate and make contemporary such concepts and the reasoning used to elucidate and justify them—but for the purpose of introducing a discipline, not illuminating an applied ethics decision process.

There is a second way of conceiving courses relating business to ethics in the undergraduate curriculum. As citizens, we have the responsibility to be able to subject to ethical scrutiny the effects of business activity on the quality of our lives and the effectiveness of governmental authority in keeping those effects within acceptable bounds. Hence, as an advanced undergraduate course in ethics, and after a student has been exposed to political theory, economics, social psychology, and similar fields, it may well be appropriate to offer a course in "Ethical Issues in the Role of Business in Society." The ethical basis for public regula-tion of corporate externalities, the relation of private enterprise to traditional ethical justifications of private property or of political liberty, the ethical ambiguities involved in consumer choice and their relation to truth in advertising—such problems as these are and will continue to be major issues not only for managers but also for social policy choice.

But the ability to wrestle with these issues as they arise within the constraints and possibilities of a managerial role when spe-cific decisions are required is, we believe, a quite different and much more specific process requiring a quite different focus to ethical instruction.

D. Business Management Schools

Professional schools are places where the general principles and methodologies of liberal learning are sharpened and transformed into tools for professional practice. The actual application and integration of these tools in management decision does not occur here, of course. This will occur only when managerial responsibility appears on the job, in an institution. But, in fact, considerable "simulation" occurs in professional school training. "Case method" pedagogy (often the only method used in management courses) assumes that learning to apply managerial tools involves more than a casuistry of deducing specific aspects of general disciplinary concepts and methodologies. The metaphor of "sharpening and focusing" is better than "deducing or deriving corollaries." And this sharpening involves so complex and rich a combination of judgment and integration—*activities* of the mind, not passive reception and rote learning—that simulation is necessary.

Ideally, courses in business ethics taught in business schools should have as prerequisites either a basic course in ethics (be it the history of ethics or methods and sources in ethics) or a remedial "short course" similar to those often required of students in other professional school courses which essentially depend on a discipline for their base. Any business ethics curriculum which takes seriously Kant's assertion that examples sometimes impair precision of intellectual insight should attempt to ensure that students "understand" rudimentary ethics skills. But care should be taken to ensure that students do not confuse the process of conceptual clarification with the quite different intellectual task of learning how to make and implement an ethical judgment in a managerial context.

Hence, we believe the basic business ethics course should begin with a brief review of the issues discussed in section I. But very quickly cases should be used to initiate the class discussion. Materials from ethics which focus on the particular concepts or reasoning patterns required to address the cases serve as background reading or case notes. In our view, the cases would not be arranged either to illustrate ethical concepts or to address "hot topics" in ethical debate. There is no way to preordain ethics topics for the diverse spheres of business responsibility which students will enter.

Instead, we believe the cases should illustrate the kinds of problems encountered in each of the eight areas where the market alone is no longer sufficient (see pp. 16–17) and they should also require the student to come to grips with some of the major kinds of judgments that confront a manager trying to alter a managerial situation.

We are thinking here of instances in which a manager has to make an instantaneous moral decision as distinguished from those that involve such basic strategic and policy implications that the company proceeds toward the decision deliberately and with care; cases that exhibit a clear conflict of values between the organization and the culture in which it functions, as distinguished from cases where there are competing claimants who share the same values but have different interests; cases that involve issues of social harm where those responsible have to self-regulate because government requirements do not exist and are not expected, as distinguished from cases where the law specifies required action (including those where the law apparently requires "unethical" practice); cases where the manager must weigh virtually certain, specific, short-term human need vs. probable, but not certain, long-term general, adverse effects on human welfare; cases where a manager can gain the support of his or her organization for ethical activity only by delaying remedial action of harmful practice or can proceed immediately to ameliorate it, but only by causing organizational disruption; cases in which a corporation can specify sharp rules without exceptions to deal with one ethical problem (and thus leave employees without options) or can issue general rules and rely on employee discretion, but then risk employee misunderstanding or circumvention. Many of these cases would have to be developed as a "series" to catch the managerial dynamic as it develops over time.

If our description of management has been accurate, it is cases that exhibit the range of *types* of moral dilemmas that will sharpen ethics in ways that help cultivate moral judgment in managerial decisionmaking. Yet, in advocating the importance of cases for management school ethics courses, we want to distinguish our view of this pedagogical method from some other approaches at two points. First, we take seriously Whitehead's suggestion not only that students must already be practiced in connecting details with general principles but also that they should be encouraged to engage in the "imaginative reconstruction" of the various principles underlying their prospective career. Hence, the careful development of case notes is extremely important. They should be designed to press students creatively to attempt to discern precisely why, for example, "market ethics" are not adequate; what mediating ethical concepts are required and what is the proper scope of their application; what redefinition of the responsibilities of the corporation are appropriate in light of the issues raised by the case. And the teacher should be concerned both to ensure that students understand the presuppositions they bring to the case, that the moral issue is properly identified, and that the reasoning process is adequate to ensure that the student is able to justify his or her decision. Students thus should be helped by the cases to explore and learn to reason through the new issues at all three levels of the individual-corporation-society relationship.[57] Additionally, cases and case teaching should proceed in such a way as to help the student see that a good analysis of an issue is never enough. Students should be given a taste of the realities and difficulties involved in implementing an ethical decision in a managerial context.

A second approach to ethical training in management schools which we see as a complement to, rather than a substitute for, a business ethics course takes seriously the argument that "We need to teach ethics in all our courses." But teaching ethics as part of other courses is not simple and will require careful development. For example, an ethics teacher could review cases in various other courses and then devote one or two class periods to teaching a "finance," or "organizational-behavior," or "production" case as an ethics case. The advantage of doing this would be to put in perspective the similarities and differences in reasoning available to address the "same case" and then to determine how the two approaches could be integrated. A similar approach might also be used in the basic ethics course, e.g., the organizational behavior or production professor teaching an "ethics" case involving complex issues in organizational dynamics or the imperatives of production efficiency.[58]

Finally, some business management schools attempt to integrate all management school disciplines under the rubric of "advanced business policy" or "general management." The efforts here are to try to bring together the skills acquired to address the full complement of management tasks—to help the student integrate the professional training experience before stepping into a management role. Most ask the student to assume the role of the chief executive officer and to relate various issues to the development of a comprehensive corporate strategy. A major focus of these courses are the points of interaction between the public and private sectors as they shape the manager's job. Major cases involving multiple decisions made over time are increasingly being developed for such courses. All of these characteristics of policy or general management courses suggest to us that such courses could provide an excellent locus for beginning to integrate moral judgment with the other skills of competent management.

E. Ethics Training for the Middle Manager

As we have pointed out, the stimulation of the moral imagination is not only the first goal of teaching ethics, it is also the most extraordinarily difficult for managers to achieve. But managers do have experience or, in Kant's term, "practice": they are aware of and know how decisions are made and under what kinds of restraints. They know also an additional and essential thing foreign to anyone outside the institution: What are the values of the institution? How does the "character" of the institution in which they manage permit or exclude ethical considerations? Precisely how does that character shape what is ethically possible in their managerial role? If management is an organ of an institution, institutional values are the "spirit" of the organization which gives it life, direction, and cohesion (or the lack thereof).

We suspect that the best way both to stimulate and awaken the moral imagination of the practicing manager is to make sure that all important aspects of an institution's character get adequate attention and to help the manager develop the tools to clarify the values, implicit and explicit, real and professed, which are at work in the institution which he or she manages.[59]

From such a beginning, managers can then be enabled to relate subsequent case material, not to business in general, but to their own business and managerial responsibilities. What may be lacking, of course, is the prior training in the analytical skills to make these cases more than anecdotal and instead capable of disciplining thought and of providing guidance for analogous situations.[60] Again, if cases are organized to exhibit types of ethical dilemmas and not as topics they may help demonstrate the need for, and give relevance to, more disciplined analytical skills development. But it is essential, then, that the course or seminar return to cases similar to those actually faced by participant managers, or else the exercise will have been reduced to a ploy to create, in Kant's terms, understanding at the expense of judgment.

In what contexts should managers be taught? An explosion in midcareer programs taught in professional management schools, and the rise of training programs for managers offered by businesses to their own employees has taken place. Ethics issues are making their way into these programs. One corporation offers a three-day ethics course to its managers (focused almost entirely on stimulating imagination and clarifying personal values), and another has its middle and top managers attend a one-week leadership training seminar which has a company-based ethics case component. Finally, one corporation has recently hired an ethicist with a business school degree, part of whose responsibility is to develop an ethics training program for its managers consisting of four full-day sessions, extending over a four-month period. In addition to background reading, the program involves some general company cases and participant-generated cases to be developed with the aid of the "instructor" in the periods between the four sessions.

We view all of these company efforts as preferable to the many one-day conferences on ethics offered by trade associations, consultants, and university alumni groups, almost all of which are both topical and superficial. To expect to cover ethics in a day is to miss entirely the dynamics we have described.

F. Ethics for Top Management

For the middle manager, the institutional history and ethos is normally perceived to be a restraint on whether ethics is thinkable. It takes considerable effort for a middle manager to see the altering of that ethos as either a responsibility or a possibility. But for the senior manager, and especially the chief executive officer, the altering of the institutional culture and ethos to complement and support the corporate strategy is increasingly seen as one of the most important management tasks. When in his *Harvard Business Review* article, Kenneth Andrews raised the question, "Can the Best Corporations by Made Moral?"[61] he turned directly to the activities of the chief executive.

For the student learning business policy, the assumption of the "administrative point of view" is a way of pulling together the threads of management preparation. For the chief executive, it can be the day-to-day challenge of discovering the capacity of various control mechanisms, policy-decision processes, promotion criteria, and so on, which open for the rest of management the "space" for ethical decision and the orientation toward the use of that space which keeps alive both the firm's economic performance and steady improvement of its social impacts.[62]

We believe that the greatest wisdom on these issues resides with the chief executives whose companies, over a period of years, maintain public credibility and ethical stature. It is they who will be able to provide the relevant case material. The combination of example, new approaches to policy decision, and organizational design which ethically successful CEO's have employed require wider recognition. Successful ethical practice is normally success in *avoiding* the hard cases where the moral choices are tragic ones and the media rushes in. But there is, of course, also much to be learned from the more plentiful examples when managers fail to create the conditions that yield ethical practice.

Few top executives will have delineated their judgment process in terms of the six capacities we have discussed. Thus the ethics teacher should be skillful at teasing out the ways in which those capacities are integrated in judgments that have altered a corporate ethos over time. CEO's and others need to see that these examples are a source of general characteristics which can be employed in other situations or corporations. For this reason, we believe that the emphasis of business ethics training for top management is almost the complete reverse of the appropriate pedagogy for undergraduates. It begins with a focus on the integrated use of management skills and proceeds back to explore the elements that made the integration possible, or, put differently, it uses experience as the way to recreate imagination.

IV: Resources and Prospects

A. Materials and Teachers: Ideals and Probabilities

This essay has analyzed both ethics and management to determine what their relationship means for teaching business ethics. But inevitably, a question must be raised as to the resources available to carry out such a program: Who can teach such courses; what materials will they use?

B. Business Ethics Teachers

Like any "underdeveloped" field, the issue of who will teach business ethics involves a chicken and egg problem. Pedagogical excellence requires good teachers; good teachers require for their development good materials and exemplary pedagogues. The problem is similar to the dilemma that the bioethics field faced ten years ago. In bioethics, the most successful initial efforts were made by ethicists, many of whom were willing to devote themselves to countless hours of clinical exposure (e.g., hospital grand rounds) to ethical problems confronting the medical profession. As the concepts and reasoning processes began to emerge, medical practitioners themselves became more' skilled in using them. The field is now blessed with some very able teachers from both fields. But as we conceive it, the primary tasks of bioethics involved the modification of available norms to changing problems in medicine and the medical profession. We suspect that the development of excellent business ethics teachers will be more difficult for all the reasons outlined in section I. More than a modification of norms is needed to synthesize this field.

If we are really talking about a new paradigm, we rather expect that the field awaits scholars who, drawing upon an understanding of ethics and management or management disciplines imaginatively construct the field and develop a curricular approach which others emulate. In other words, what Fritz Roethlisberger did with and for the field of organizational behavior is needed in business ethics. Is there anything that can be done to prepare the way?[63]

Derek Bok has treated this issue generally in trying to provide guidance for the training of teachers in applied ethics fields. He specified three prerequisites for teachers in applied ethics which seem applicable to business ethics teachers. What is needed, he suggests, is persons who have: (1) an adequate knowledge of moral philosophy; (2) knowledge of the field of human affairs to which their course is addressed; and (3) who are capable of conducting rigorous class discussion. He found no academic program that was equipped to train a fully qualified instructor; and he suggested "serious interdisciplinary programs" focused toward training such scholars.[64] Clearly, this may help force the paradigm. We suspect, however, that progress could be made more quickly if universities provided senior scholars, in either ethics or business, encouragement and opportunity to immerse themselves as students (or even practitioners) in the "other discipline." In our view this would be the ideal, but even this envisages a period of development.

At the moment, then, the most critical obstacle to the teaching of ethics at business schools and elsewhere is the lack of teachers interested and competent in providing even moderately inspired business ethics instruction. Virtually all full-time faculty members of business schools are trained in one or more relatively technical areas—accounting, marketing, finance, organizational behavior, and so on. With a handful of individual exceptions, these persons are simply not able to sustain serious theoretical reflection on the ethical dimensions of business activity, even if they were so inclined.

Alternatively, even if it were advisable, it is highly unlikely that many business schools can be persuaded to hire faculty members whose formal training and experience is solely in philosophy or religion. If relatively few business schools have either the resources or the commitment to hire full-time faculty in the external environment area, they will be slow to hire a full-time ethicist, particularly since philosophy is even more remote from the traditional intellectual center of gravity of business education than is political science or law. Most business school faculty remain quite suspicious of entrusting their students to faculty members who are not knowledgeable about the "real" world of management or trained in management disciplines.

This means that, for the immediate future, ethics will most likely be taught by one of four means. First, at least some of the faculty members now teaching business and society—particularly those trained in the social sciences—can be reasonably expected to reorient at least some of their teaching and research efforts to ethical concerns. Many ethical issues are already implicit in the existing business and society curriculum; what is minimally required is that more of them be made explicit. Whether more than explication can be expected in the context of courses taught by business and society professors is unclear.

Secondly, courses can be jointly taught by a business faculty member and a faculty member whose professional training is in ethics. Team-teaching has sometimes worked well in the early development of applied ethics teaching. However, substantial effort must be exerted by both teachers to obtain a real integration of their perspectives; otherwise students will be left with the impression that they can premise their choices on either ethical or good management principles, but not both.

A third possibility is for business school students to receive credit for a course taught in the school of religion or philosophy, though this is more likely to be accepted at the undergraduate level. This model places the responsibility for integrating ethical theory with management solely on the student. It may be preferable to a poorly devised business ethics course. But it represents a substantial retreat from the approach we discussed in section III.

Finally, ethics material can be designed for inclusion in the courses that constitute the core of the traditional business school curriculum. While not all faculty members will be willing or able to encourage their students to approach their academic specialties from an ethical perspective, many might well prove quite receptive to such an approach, particularly if material were prepared for them. While perhaps least desirable from the pedagogical viewpoint, this alternative is likely to meet the least opposition from faculty members.

Similar difficulties will arise when the context of ethics training is the corporate institution itself. Many corporations draw heavily on management school faculties for their training programs; and they will, of course, have limited options for business ethics faculty for the immediate future. Some corporations rely on their own training personnel. But we know of no current efforts to develop training courses in ethics for corporate training staffs (The Society for Values in Higher Education will, however, orient part of its 1980 Institute in this direction). Finally, as discussed earlier, experiments have begun to "bring ethicists in" to corporations for this purpose—either on a consulting basis or as full-time corporate personnel. But it is clear that the dilemma of "who will teach ethics?" in the corporation itself is even more serious than in the management school.

It may reasonably be asked, then, whether business ethics should be taught at all until there emerges the synthesis—the "new paradigm" with people prepared to teach it—that allows the field to begin to realize the potential we believe it has. But new disciplines never emerge "full grown"; they emerge tortuously whenever new knowledge requires transmission or societal transitions require learned treatment. Ethics *is* a well-established discipline, and the difficulty business ethics presents is the integration of the methods of ethics with a rapidly changing institutional context. If this is remembered, and teachers struggling to come to terms with it do so with academic seriousness, their less than perfect starts should be as tolerable as they are in the developing stages of other disciplines and in efforts to reconstruct fields where traditional methods and materials have been superseded by changes.

There is another point: we are persuaded that the growing literature in the business ethics field is beginning to provide the "elements" of the needed reconstruction and that the business and society field has already received benefits from the clarification which these elements afford. Many of these materials are listed in the attached bibliography, though the reader will note the dearth of material linking "mediating ethical concepts" to business situations or decisions. Even less numerous are "cases" which illustrate the kinds of dilemmas which we suggested would be most helpful.

C. Materials

These gaps in materials suggest another fruitful avenue for teacher preparation in business ethics: research. There have recently been studies of the attitudes of business people to ethical issues.[65] But to our knowledge, almost no effort has been made to determine what role ethical discourse plays in actual managerial decisionmaking or how mechanisms and policies being devised to improve the ethical character of corporate institutions actually work. There are ethics case materials now appearing in business ethics texts,[66] but most of these reflect the proclivity to see ethics as involving hard cases of the "head in the hands" variety.

We believe that one step would involve a sustained research program carefully designed to examine corporate decision processes in what we have suggested are the eight areas of corporate activity where market ethics alone are not adequate. Examples of such research topics will help:

1. Ambiguous government requirements: (a) the decisionmaking discourse of several companies attempting to determine whether or not to participate in a "voluntary wage and price restraint" program being advocated by the federal government; (b) the process employed by a company attempting to establish internal mechanisms to monitor and then certify to the government that under the Toxic Substances Control Act its products do not cause an unreasonable risk to health.

2. Influencing public policy: (a) the testimony preparation decision process of several companies responding to onerous proposed regulations from, for example, the Environmental Protection Agency; (b) the policy selection process of a company deciding whether or not to advocate that Congress keep on the

books a tax deduction which is advantageous to the company but will not, in fact, alter its investment patterns.

3. Activities in overlapping jurisdictions: (a) the decision process of companies attempting to set a transfer price in a situation where the tax codes of the exporting and importing country differ; (b) the policymaking process of a company trying to decide whether to export from a European subsidiary a strategic product whose export from the United States is proscribed by U.S. law.

4. Sales of potentially injurious products: (a) the decisionmaking process of a corporate engineering group trying to decide whether to inform a governmental authority about a product that poses a potential risk to consumer safety which has not been contemplated in existing regulation; (b) a policy debate on alternative mechanisms to encourage employee reporting of safety or health risks to the quality-assurance staff or to top management.

5. Cessation of a product or function: (a) the decisionmaking process of companies attempting to determine when and how to inform employees about a plant relocation and what kinds of benefits and reemployment services to provide these employees; (b) the policymaking process concerning the level of parts inventory to build as the company withdraws its products from participation in a market segment.

6. Internal company policies: (a) the ethical language used in the decision process to determine levels of privacy protection to be incorporated in newly computerized employee records; (b) the decisions made by a company as to whether employees should be required to certify that neither they nor any of their colleagues have violated the company's ethical practices policy.

7. Policies in surrounding communities: the evaluation of a company's policy concerning whether employees will be encouraged to take responsible positions in community organizations and whether they will or will not be asked (explicitly or implicitly) to represent company positions within these organizations.

Each of these examples represents fertile ground for descriptive research on ethics in businesses. Each could be developed as a "case" or "case series" to which case notes on ethical concepts or reasoning could be appended. And, alternatively, each could be a part of a research project on comparative approaches to ethical management decision and to the mechanisms and the processes used.

Once this descriptive research begins to yield data, it could give rise to relational research or research that links results to causative factors in organizational dynamics or types of industries. We are thinking of studies to analyze: Is the moral reasoning process typically different when top management is involved in ethical decisions? What role do legal departments typically play in such discussions? Do managers whose background includes training in other professions (engineering, law, design, etc.) approach ethical questions differently from those trained in general management? What really "happens" to the manager who expresses strong personal convictions on ethical issues that are different from those of the organization or its top decisionmaker? Does the ethical discourse on these issues differ when an organization is highly centralized or decentralized? Are there any statistically significant differences in the way in which these issues are decided or discussed in consumer-oriented as distinguished from "supplier" companies or subsidiaries? When in discussion of an ethical issue do managers feel it necessary to justify their decisions in terms of long-term economic performance or in terms of the public relations implications (will the company be shamed in public?) as distinguished from a direct appeal to human welfare or ethical principle? Is the ethical discourse of a highly profitable company significantly different from one with low margins which is under intense competitive pressure? Data on these issues would importantly add to the business ethics teachers' understanding of the possibilities and constraints in the several contexts in which their students will be trying to exercise moral judgment. And as it developed, this data would also be generating instructive course material (both cases and analytical materials).

Research of this sort will be much more difficult to carry out than the usual business research. It will almost surely involve more direct observance by the researcher of the managerial process than is typical. And in addition, it will involve cooperation with company managements, for the researcher will in most cases need to be advised of an impending decision and not await its publicly celebrated outcome.

D. Business Ethics and the Business Community

This discussion of needed research and ethics case material leads into a final issue: Is the business community itself seriously enough concerned with corporate ethics to make available information about its processes in this area? To put the question more generally, is the business community really prepared to support the study of business ethics? It is one thing to argue, as we did in section I, that the competent managers will need ethics in the eighties. It is another to say that the business community will so value ethics training that it will actively encourage development of the field.

On this point, difficult judgments will have to be made by those who advocate the development of business ethics. Like any applied ethics field, business ethics seeks reform and the improvement of institutional and individual practice. To this extent, business ethics will be seen by some as subversive.[67] On the other hand, business ethics can the be used to legitimate dubious practices by providing explanations in defense of wrongful activity. Every professional school is tempted to please the present members of the profession by submerging the reformatory implications of its pedagogy. Ethics is particularly vulnerable to this temptation. And yet the future management of business institutions will not be served by ethics teaching that pronounces censorious judgments from the outside or that becomes so absorbed in corporate dilemmas that it loses critical distance.

In our view, perhaps the single greatest long-term challenge to business ethics is the task of maintaining a balance between empathy for the ethical complexity of managerial choice and the independence to render effective criticism. The prospects for maintaining that balance finally depend, we believe, on whether ethics teaching merely focuses on specific "hot topics" in business ethics or on the development of the capacity for moral judgment in management. If the focus is on the former, then depending on the predilections of the instructor, ethics will become either a good context for public relations training or for ad hominem censure of corporate institutions. If, however, the attention is focused on the qualities and skills necessary for mature judgment in management contexts, the field can develop with an integrity which will command the respect of all serious members and observers of the business community.

Hence, we see the need for thoughtful and sustained cooperation between management schools and the corporate sector as this field evolves. If we are right about the challenges of the eighties, then the self-interest of both school and corporation lie in effective collaboration to help this field develop.

Notes

1. G. J. Warnock, *Contemporary Moral Philosophy* (New York: St. Martin's Press, 1967).

2. Peter Drucker, *Management: Tasks, Responsibilities, and Practices* (New York: Harper & Row, 1974), p. 37.

3. Ibid., p. 39.

4. Take, for example, changes that occur in the medical profession as society changes. Self-determination is a concept that has increasingly "made its way" into human health decisions. As a result, "informed patient consent" has reduced the sphere in which physicians alone make decisions about what is the appropriate health care for their patients. These changes have caused complex reexamination of the physician's role as well as the meaning of both "health" and "healing." But healing remains at once the central purpose of a physician's practice and its primary normative guide.

5. The failure of traditional market theory to explain and control managerial discretion was documented as early as 1932 by Adolf Berle and C. Gardiner Means in *The Modern Corporation and Private Property,* (New York: New York Commerce Clearing House Inc., 1932). See also Merrick Dodd, "For Whom Are Corporate Managers Trustees?" *Harvard Business Review* 45 (1932), 1145–63; Adolf Berle, "For Whom Corporate Managers Are Trustees," *Harvard Business Review* 45 (1932), 1365–72; Dodd, "Is Effective Enforcement of Fiduciary Duties of Corporate Managers Practicable," *University of Chicago Law Review* 2 (1933), 194–207; Berle, "Corporate Powers as Powers in Trust," *Harvard Business Review* 45 (1937), 1049–74.

For contemporary debates about managerial power and responsibility, see Theodore Levitt, "The Dangers of Social Responsibility," *Harvard Business Review,* September-October, 1956; Sumner Slichter, "A Defense of Bigness in Business," *New York Times Magazine,* August 4, 1957; numerous defenses of "managerialism," such as James C. Worthy's *Big Business and Free Men,* (New York: Harper & Brothers, Publishers, 1959). A now classic collection by

Edward S. Mason is an appropriate starting point for understanding the continuing theoretical gaps in our economic structure which set the stage for considerations of ethical management: *The Corporation in Modern Society,* (New York: Atheneum, 1966).

6. The complex debate about this issue is summarized, and in our view resolved, in John G. Simon et al., *The Ethical Investor,* New Haven, 1972, chap. 2.

7. Milton Friedman himself seems to acknowledge this, though his interpretation of what is required is almost cynical and, in our view, likely to be ineffective. "The Social Responsibility of Business Is To Increase Its Profits," *New York Times Magazine,* July 7, 1970, p. 32.

8. See Peter Berger, et al., *The Homeless Mind: Modernization and Consciousness* (New York: Random House, 1973).

9. Shenefield leads into these conclusions by reciting certain factors which directly relate to the experience of many Americans, such as loss of commitment to local communities, and the economic impact on communities in which plants are closed because, although viable, they do not achieve bottom-line management goals. Testimony of John H. Shenefield, Assistant Attorney General, Antitrust Division, before the Senate Committee on the Judiciary, concerning conglomerate mergers, March 8, 1979.

10. And these new liabilities may extend beyond the organization to the manager or the director. There is a growing body of literature, and some new case law, on various aspects of this new approach. See Christopher Stone, *Where The Law Ends,* (New York: Harper & Row, 1975), pp. 144–45; 204–6; and Tony McAdams and Robert Miljus, "Growing Criminal Liability of Executives," *Harvard Business Review*, March–April 1977, pp. 36–58.

11. Alfred North Whitehead, *The Aims of Education* (New York: Macmillan, 1929), p. 94.

12. Quoted in Walter Kiechel III, "Harvard Business School Restudies Itself," *Fortune*, June 18, 1979, p. 58.

13. Frank Pierson et al., *The Education of American Businessmen* (New York: McGraw-Hill, 1959); Robert Aaron Gordon and James Edwin Howell, *Higher Education for Business* (New York: Columbia University Press, 1959).

14. Pierson et al., p. 334.

15. Quoted in *Business and Society Curriculum: A Position Paper,* prepared by the Governance Committee of the Social Issues in Management Division, the Academy of Management, January, 1976.

16. Gordon and Howell, p. 22.

17. George A. Steiner, *Proposal for Course,* UCLA, Schools of Business Administration, Division of Research, August 17, 1962, p. 1.

18. *Educating Tomorrow's Manager,* Committee for Economic Development, 1964.

19. AACSB Accreditation Council, *Policies, Procedures and Standards, 1976–77,* pp. 30–32.

20. For a discussion of the ethical and social pressures confronting management in the mid-seventies and the confusions they created for executives, see Leonard Silk and David Vogel, *Ethics and Profits: The Crisis of Confidence in American Business* (New York: Simon and Schuster, 1976).

21. *Business and Society Curriculum,* p. 3.

22. Ibid.

23. Earl F. Cheit, "What is the Field of Business and Society and Where Is It Going?" In Edwin M. Epstein and Dow Votaw eds., *Legitimacy, Responsibility, Rationality* (Santa Monica: Goodyear, 1978), pp. 183–302.

24. William Frederick, "Business and Society Curriculum: Suggested Guidelines for Accreditation," *AACSB Bulletin,* Spring, 1977.

25. George Steiner, "University Courses in the Business Society Area," *Contemporary Challenges in the Business Society Relationship,* Los Angeles: Graduate School of Management, UCLA, 1972.

26. Kirk Hansen, "Business Schools Make Room for Corporate Social Policy," *Business and Society Review/Innovation,* Summer, 1973, pp. 75–81.

27. Thomas F. McMahon, *Report on the Teaching of Socio-Ethical Issues In Collegiate Schools of Business/Public Administration,* Center for the Study of Applied Ethics, University of Virginia, 1975.

28. Robert Holloway and Delbert C. Hastings, "The Business and Society Course and Its Discontents." Working Paper no. 44, College of Business Administration, University of Minnesota, 1978.

29. Rogene Buchholz, *Business Environment/Public Policy; A Study of Teaching and Research in Schools of Business and Management.* Center for the Study of American Business, Working Paper no. 41, 1979.

30. Statement concerning Curriculum Standard IVb, AACSB, prepared for presentation to the Standards Committee. AACSB, Committee on Curriculum and Standards, Division of Social Issues in Management. Academy of Management. p. 7.

31. Ibid., p. 3.

32. *Business and Society Curriculum,* p. 8.

33. Ibid., p. 10, 15.

34. Buchholz, pp. 109–10.

35. McMahon, pp. 110–11.

36. Kirk Hansen, p. 76.

37. Andrew Mann, "The Ethics Puzzle," *MBA*, September, 1974, pp. 23–26.

38. Directory of Corporate Social Policy Courses in Graduate Business School or the Professors Who Teach Them, NACBS, unpublished, October 1, 1974.

39. William Frederick, "Education for Social Responsibility: What the Schools Are Doing about it," *Liberal Education* 63, no. 2 (May, 1977), p. 193.

40. Buchholz, p. 99.

41. For more information, write Norman E. Bowie, Director, Center for the Study of Values, Department of Philosophy, University of Delaware, Newark, Delaware, 19711.

42. For more information, write David Smith, Executive Director, Society for Values in Higher Education, 363 St. Ronan Street, New Haven, Connecticut 06511.

43. For reports on the first two conferences, see *Business Ethics Report,* Highlights of Bentley College's First Annual Conference on Business Ethics and *Business Ethics Report,* Highlights of Bentley College's Second National Conference on Business Ethics. Available from the Center for Business Ethics at Bentley College, Beaver and Forrest Streets, Waltham, Mass. 02154.

44. See Bibliography for complete citation.

45. See Bibliography for complete citation.

46. Derek Bok, "The President's Report," *John Harvard's Journal,* May-June, 1979, p. 80. For a discussion of some of the controversy provoked by Bok's criticism of Harvard's exclusive reliance on the case method, see Kiechell, "Harvard Business School. . .," pp. 48–50, 53, 54, 57, 58.

47. Bok, p. 80.

48. Immanuel Kant, *Critique of Pure Reason,* trans. by N.K. Smith (New York: St. Martin's Press, 1961), pp. 172–78.

49. These elements closely parallel the five goals for the teaching of ethics generally specified in *The Teaching of Ethics in Higher Education: A Report by The Hastings Center* (Hastings-on-Hudson, N.Y.: The Hastings Center, 1980). In what follows we have frequently simply specified its concerns for the managerial context.

50. John K. Galbraith, *American Capitalism, The Concept of Countervailing Power* (New York: Houghton, Mifflin, 1955).

51. Kenneth R. Andrews, "Can the Best Corporations Be Made Moral?" in *Harvard Business Review,* May–June, 1973, p. 60.

52. As Henry D. Aiken asserts, i.e., that at the highest level of moral

discourse, "Decision is King." *The Levels of Moral Discourse* (New York: Alfred A. Knopf, 1962), p. 87.

53. Kant, *Critique of Pure Reason*.

54. Ibid.

55. Alfred North Whitehead, *The Aims of Education and Other Essays* (New York: Macmillan, 1929), p. 96.

56. We distinguish here between undergraduate programs in the "liberal arts" tradition and those which directly prepare students for managerial responsibility. For the latter, an amalgam of the approaches we suggest for undergraduate and professional school ethics courses would have to be attempted.

57. We are impressed with the similarities between what we are suggesting and the way Fritz Roethlisberger developed the case method for his organizational behavior courses. In fact, we suspect that courses in ethics closely patterned after the Roethlisberger model would be an excellent first step toward the kind of course we envisage. Roethlisberger, too, found that he had to develop cases in quite different ways from those of his predecessors and colleagues. See *The Elusive Phenomena* (Cambridge, Mass.: Harvard University Press, 1977). p. 123–42.

58. Roethlisberger's suggestions on this point are particularly interesting. He typically "outlawed" student solutions to cases that involved radical corporate reorganizations or postulated changes in motivation or personality. The tendency for students to "wave a wand" over a complex organizational problem vitiates the rationale for case teaching. Ibid., p. 128.

59. One of the authors recently co-convened a two-week seminar of managers and ethics teachers which began in this manner. The approach was clearly superior to earlier experiences of beginning with ethical treatises or problems or even cases. The managers proved increasingly adept at describing the interplay of their institution's history, leadership, the product or service provided, industry role, etc., in shaping these values and in projecting how they would evolve over time. These practitioners reported that they had never before given serious thought to the question and that many of their own problems in trying to manage effectively were quickly clarified. In addition, by having given attention to institutional values first, the practitioners were not only more open to the possibility that they lived in a web of moral relationships, but vigorously explored—and effectively related—the analytical materials introduced later in the course.

60. This will be true for some time to come. We suspect that a small minority of business people have had ethics training in their undergraduate programs; we know that a tiny minority have taken the uneven business ethics courses just now beginning to be offered. And their closest analogue, business and society courses, have become regular curricula for business students only during the past few years.

61. Andrews, "Can the Best Corporations Be Made Moral?" pp. 57–64.

62. See Henry B. Schacht's address to the "Project on Corporate Responsibilty," a Spring Hill Center Conference, November 15–16, 1977 (unpublished).

63. A preliminary effort in this direction will be available in Bradshaw, Thornton and Vogel, David, eds. *Corporations and Their Critics* (New York: McGraw-Hill, 1980).

64. "Can Ethics Be Taught?" *Change*, October 1978, p. 30.

65. See Bibliography, sections II and III.

66. Thomas, Donaldson and Werhane, Patricia, eds., *Ethical Issues in Business: A Philosophical Approach* (Englewood Cliffs, N.J.: Prentice-Hall, 1979); and Beauchamp Tom and Bowie, Norman, eds., *Ethical Theory and Business* (Englewood Cliffs, N.J.: Prentice-Hall, 1979).

67. See, for example, Irving Kristol, "Business Ethics," *Wall Street Journal*, July 12, 1979.

Bibliography

I. An Introductory Note

Three recently published textbooks are explicitly concerned with business ethics: Tom Beauchamp and Norman Bowie, eds. *Ethical Theory and Business* (Englewood Cliffs, N.J.: Prentice-Hall, 1979); Thomas Donaldson and Patricia Werhane, eds. *Ethical Issues in Business: A Philosophical Approach* (Englewood Cliffs, N.J.: Prentice-Hall, 1979); and Vincent Barry, *Moral Issues in Business* (Belmont Calif.: Wadsworth Publishing Co., 1979). Each includes discussions of ethical issues from a philosophical perspective, case studies of ethical problems confronting business, and contemporary articles on business and society. Although they represent the first efforts to link the philosophical study of ethical concepts and theories with the problems of business, neither addresses the issues in the way we have suggested in section I.

Numerous readers, which give a fairly comprehensive overview of issues covered in business and society courses, are available. Most consist of a combination of case studies and selections from books, journals, and magazines. While only some of the issues covered directly raise ethical concerns, most can readily be discussed in an ethical context. These readers include:

Ackerman, Robert and Bauer, Raymond, eds. *Corporate Social Responsiveness: The Modern Dilemma.* Reston, Va.: Reston Publishing Company, Inc., 1976.

Steiner, George A. and Steiner, John F., eds. *Issues in Business and Society.* New York: Random House, Inc., 1972.

Nicholson, Edward A., Litschert, Robert J., and Anthony, William P., eds. *Business Responsibility and Social Issues.* Columbus, Ohio: Charles E. Merrill Publishing Company, 1974.

Ermann, M. David and Lundman, Richard J., eds. *Corporate and Governmental Deviance: Problems of Organizational Behavior in Contemporary Society.* New York: Oxford University Press, Inc., 1978.

Barach,. Jeffrey A., ed. *The Individual, Business, and Society.* Englewood Cliffs, N.J.: Prentice-Hall, 1977.

Luthans, Fred and Hodgetts, Richard M., eds. *Social Issues In Business.* New York: Macmillan Co., 1976.

Carroll, Archie, ed. *Managing Corporate Social Responsibility.* Boston: Little, Brown, 1977.

The case studies distributed by the Intercollegiate Case Clearing House, Soldiers Field P.O., Boston, Mass. 02163, are a useful source of teaching material. These cases are continually being updated and cover a wide variety of areas including personal ethics, social responsibility, and corporate ethics. Various other collections of case studies include:

Hay, Robert, Gray, Edmund and Gates, James, eds. *Business and Society.* Cincinnati, Ohio: South-Western Publishing Co., 1976.

Heilbroner, Robert, ed. *In the Name of Profit.* New York: Warner Paperback, 1973.

Hodgetts, Richard M. *The Business Enterprise: Social Challenge, Social Response.* Philadelphia, Pa.: W.B. Saunders Co., 1977.

Sethi, S. Prakash. *Up Against the Corporate Wall.* Englewood Cliffs, N.J.: Prentice-Hall, 1971.

Business and Society Review, a quarterly published in New York, frequently contains articles discussing contemporary ethical problems confronting business, as well as material on the teaching of ethics at business schools. Many of its articles are appropriate for classroom use. *Fortune* magazine also often contains articles ideal for distribution to students. Several useful collections of original essays address both ethical and social issues, almost all of which are based on conference proceedings. They include:

Cheit, Earl, ed. *The Business Establishment.* New York: John Wiley & Sons, 1964.

Clarence, Walton. *The Ethics of Corporate Conduct.* Englewood Cliffs, N.J.: Prentice-Hall, 1977.

De George, Richard T. and Pichler, Joseph A. *Ethics, Free Enterprise, and Public Policy: Original Essays on Moral Issues in Business.* New York: Oxford University Press, 1978.

Epstein, Edwin and Votaw, Dow, eds. *Legitimacy, Responsibility and Rationality.* Santa Monica: Goodyear, 1978.

McKie, James, ed. *Social Responsibility and the Business Predicament.* Washington, D.C.: Brookings, 1974.

Nader, Ralph and Green, Mark, eds. *Corporate Power in America.* New York: Grossman, 1973.

Sethi, S. Prakash. *The Unstable Ground: Corporate Social Policy in a Dynamic Society.* New York: Melville, 1974.

In 1978, Lee Preston published *Research in Corporate Social Performance and Policy* (JAI Press), the first of a series of annual volumes presenting current research by academics, most of whom teach in the business and society field. There is one published bibliography dealing with business ethics:

Jones, Donald G. *A Bibliography of Business Ethics, 1971–1975.* Charlottesville, Va.: University Press of Virginia, 1977.

In addition, the Center for Business Ethics at Bentley College, Waltham, Massachusetts 02154, has prepared an extensive bibliography of books and articles on business ethics, which is updated periodically. Copies are available from the Center.

II. Business Ethics—An Overview

Books

Gothie, Daniel L. ed. *Business Ethics and Social Responsibilities: Theory and Practice.* Charlottesville, Va.: University of Virginia Press, 1974.

Hill, Ivan. *The Ethical Basis of Economic Freedom.* Chapel Hill, N.C.: American Viewpoint, Inc., 1976.

Kugel, Yerachmiel, and Gruenberg, Gladys W., eds. *Ethical Perspectives on Business and Society*. Lexington, Mass.: D. C. Heath and Company, 1977.

Silk, Leonard, and Vogel, David. *Ethics and Profits*. New York: Simon & Schuster, 1976.

Southard, Samuel. *Ethics for Executives*. New York: Cornerstone, 1977.

Articles

Carr, Albert Z. "Is Business Bluffing Ethical?" *Harvard Business Review,* January-February 1968.

Purcell, Theodore. "A Practical Guide to Ethics in Business," *Business and Society Review* 13 (Spring 1975), pp. 43–50.

Ways, Max. "Business Faces Growing Pressures to Behave Better," *Fortune,* May 1974.

III. The Practice of Business Ethics

Books

Garrett, Thomas M., Baumhart, Raymond C., Purcell, Theodore V. and Roets, Perry. *Cases in Business Ethics*. New York: Appleton-Century-Crofts, 1968.

Articles

Brenner, Steven N. and Molander, Earl A. "Is the Ethics of Business Changing?" *Harvard Business Review*, January–February 1977, pp. 57–71.

Faber, Eberhard. "How I Lost Our Great Debate about Corporate Ethics," *Fortune,* November 1976.

Kramer, Otto P. "Ethics Programs Can Help Companies Set Standards of Conduct," *Administrative Management* 38, no. 1 (January 1977), pp. 46 ff.

IV. The Individual and The Organization

Books

Ewing, David W. *Freedom Inside the Organization*. New York: E. P. Dutton, 1977.

Nader, Ralph et al., eds. *Whistle-Blowing–The Nader Report*. New York: Harper & Row, 1975.

Stone, Christopher. *Where the Law Ends*. New York: Harper & Row, 1975.

Articles

Carr, Albert Z. "Can an Executive Afford a Conscience?" *Harvard Business Review*, July–August 1970.

Hanan, Mack. "Make Way for the New Organization Man," *Harvard Business Review*, July–August 1971.

McAdams, Tony, and Miljus, Robert. "Growing Criminal Liability of Executives, *Harvard Business Review*, March–April 1977, pp. 36–58.

Walters, Kenneth. "Your Employees' Right to Blow the Whistle," *Harvard Business Review*, July–August 1971.

V. Corporate Social Responsibility—Principles

Books

Blumberg, Phillip I. *Corporate Responsibility in a Changing Society*. Boston, Mass.: Boston University School of Law, 1972.

Chamberlain, Neil W. *The Limits of Corporate Responsibility*. New York: Basic Books, 1973.

Articles

Andrews, Kenneth R. "Can the Best Corporations be Made Moral?" *Harvard Business Review*, May–June 1973, pp. 57–64.

Friedman, Milton. "The Social Responsibility of Business Is to Increase Its Profits," *The New York Times Magazine*, September 13, 1970.

Levitt, Theodore. "The Dangers of Social Responsibility," *Harvard Business Review*, September–October 1958, pp. 41–50.

Votaw, Dow. "Genius Becomes Rare: A Comment of the Doctrine of Social Responsibility, pt. 1," (part 2, Spring 1973), *California Management Review* 15, no. 2 (Winter 1972), pp. 25–31.

VI. Corporate Social Responsibility—Practice

Books

Ackerman, R. W. *The Social Challenge to Business*. Cambridge, Mass.: Harvard University Press, 1975.

Anshen, Melvin, ed. *Managing the Socially Responsible Corporation*. New York: Macmillan Company, 1974.

Bradshaw, Thornton and Vogel, David, eds. *Corporations and Their Critics: Issues and Answers or the Problems of Corporate Social Responsibility*. New York: McGraw-Hill, 1980.

Articles

"How Social Responsibility Became Institutionalized," *Business Week,* June 30, 1973, pp. 74–82.

McCall, David B. "Profit: Spur for Solving Social Ills," *Harvard Business Review,* May–June 1973.

Moskowitz, Milton. "Profiles in Corporate Responsibility: The Ten Worst, The Ten Best," *Business and Society Review,* Spring 1975, pp. 28–42.

VII. The Ethical Principles of a Market Economy

Books

Brozen, Yale, Johnson, Elmer W., Powers, Charles W. *Can The Market Sustain An Ethic?* Chicago: University of Chicago Press, 1978.

Friedman, Milton. *Capitalism and Freedom.* Chicago: University of Chicago Press, 1962.

Harrington, Michael. *The Twilight of Capitalism.* New York: Simon and Schuster, 1976.

Heilbroner, Robert. *The Making of Economic Society.* Englewood Cliffs, N.J.: Prentice-Hall, 1962.

Hirschman, Albert. *The Passions and the Interests.* Princeton, N.J.: Princeton University Press, 1977.

Kristol, Irving. *Two Cheers for Capitalism.* New York: Basic Books, 1978.

Lindblom, Charles E. *Politics and Markets.* New York: Free Press, 1978.

Okun, Arthur. *Equality and Efficiency.* Washington, D.C.: Brookings Institution, 1975.

Schumpeter, Joseph. *Capitalism, Socialism and Democracy.* New York: Harper & Row, 1950.

Tucker, Robert, ed. *The Marx-Engels Reader.* New York: W. W. Norton, 1972.

Weber, Max. *The Protestant Ethic and the Spirit of Capitalism.* New York: Charles Scribners Sons, 1958.

Articles

Lane, Robert E. "Autonomy, Felicity, Futility: The Effects of the Market Economy in Political Personality," *The Journal of Politics* 40 (1978), pp. 3–23.

VIII. Overseas Payments

Books

Adams, Gordon et al. *The Invisible Hand: Questionable Corporate Payments*

Overseas. New York: Council on Economic Priorities, 1976.

Basche, James R. *Unusual Foreign Payments*. New York: The Conference Board, 1976.

Jacoby, Neil H. *Bribery and Extortion: A Study of Corporate Political Payments Abroad*. New York: Macmillan Company, 1977.

Articles

Basche, James. "Those 'Questionable Payments,'" *Across the Board,* July 1977.

Griffith, Thomas. "Payoff is not 'Accepted Practice,'" *Fortune,* August 1975.

Guzzardi, Walter, Jr. "An Unscandalized View of Those 'Bribes' Abroad," *Fortune,* July 1976.

Gwirtzman, Milton S. "Is Bribery Defensible?" *The New York Times Magazine,* October 5, 1975, pp. 19ff.

Shaplen, Robert. "Lockheed in Japan" Part I," *The New Yorker,* January 23, 1978, p. 48ff.; Part II, January 30, 1978, pp. 74ff.

IX. Ethics in the Practice of Accounting

Carmichael, D. R. "Corporate Accountability and Illegal Act," *Journal of Accountancy,* January 1977, pp. 77–81.

Marshall, Juanita. "The Full Disclosure Problem," *Management Accounting,* February 1977, pp. 24–26.

Solomon, Kenneth, and Muller, Hyman. "Illegal Payments: Where the Auditor Stands," *Journal of Accountancy,* January 1977, pp. 51–57.

X. Ethics in the Practice of Marketing

Books

Aaker, David A. and Day, George S. *Consumerism: Search for the Consumer Interest*. New York: The Free Press, 1974.

Nader, Ralph. *The Consumer and Corporate Accountability*. New York: Harcourt Brace Jovanovich, 1973.

Preston, Lee E. *Social Issues in Marketing*. Glenview, Ill.: Scott, Foresman & Co., 1967.

Articles

Bowie, Mark. "Pinto Madness," *Mother Jones,* September–October 1977, pp. 18–30.

Clasen, Earl A. "Marketing Ethics and the Consumer," *Harvard Business Review,* January–February 1967, pp. 79–86.

Greenland, Leo. "Thinking Ahead: Advertisers Must Stop Conning Consumers," *Harvard Business Review,* July–August 1974.

Levitt, Theodore. "The Morality (?) of Advertising," *Harvard Business Review,* July–August 1970.

XI. Ethics in the Practice of Personnel Management

Books
Kanter, Rosabeth Moss. *Men and Women of the Corporation.* New York: Basic Books, 1977.

Purcell, Theodore V. and Cavanaugh, Gerald F. *Blacks in the Industrial World.* New York: The Free Press, 1972.

Articles
Boyle, M. Barbara. "Equal Opportunities for Women is Smart Business," *Harvard Business Review,* May–June 1973, pp. 85–95.

Fretz, C. F., and Haymen, Joanne. "Progress for Women—Men are Still More Equal," *Harvard Business Review,* September–October 1973, pp. 133–42.

"IBM's Guidelines to Employee Privacy: An Interview with Frank T. Cary," *Harvard Business Review,* September–October 1976, pp. 82–90.

XII. Ethics in the Practice of Investment

Books
Longstretch, Bevis, and Rosenbloom, H. David. *Corporate Social Responsibility and the Institutional Investor.* New York: Praeger, 1973.

Powers, Charles W. *Social Responsibility and Investment.* Nashville: Abingdon, 1971.

Simon, John G., Powers, Charles W. and Gunnemann, Jon P. *The Ethical Investor.* New Haven: Yale University Press, 1972.

Vogel, David. *Lobbying the Corporation.* New York: Basic Books, 1978.

Articles
Brown, R. Gene. "Ethical and Other Problems in Publishing Financial Forecasts," *Financial Analysts Journal,* March–April 1972.

Malkiel, Burton G., and Quandt, Richard E. "Moral Issues In Investment Policy," *Harvard Business Review,* March–April 1971.

Roberts, Keith. "The Seven Veils of Ethical Investigating," *Business and Society Review,* Fall 1976, pp. 70–72.

Sommer, A.A. Jr. "The Limits of Disclosure," *Financial Executive* 43, no. 10 (October 1975), pp. 42–54.

Publications from The Teaching of Ethics Project
The Hastings Center

A number of publications on the teaching of ethics in higher education are available from The Hastings Center. A list of these publications appears on the back cover. Return order form to: The Hastings Center, 360 Broadway, Hastings-on-Hudson, N.Y. 10706

I. **The Teaching of Ethics in Higher Education: A Report by The Hastings Center** . . . . ($5)
II. Michael J. Kelly, **Legal Ethics and Legal Education** . . . . ($4)
III. Clifford G. Christians & Catherine L. Covert, **Teaching Ethics in Journalism Education** . . . . ($4)
IV. K. Danner Clouser, **Teaching Bioethics: Strategies, Problems, and Resources** . . . . ($4)
V. Charles W. Powers & David Vogel, **Ethics in the Education of Business Managers.** . . . . ($5)
VI. Donald P. Warwick, **The Teaching of Ethics in the Social Sciences.** . . . . ($4)
VII. Robert J. Baum, **Ethics and Engineering Curricula.** . . . . ($4)
VIII. Joel L. Fleishman & Bruce L. Payne, **Ethical Dilemmas and the Education of Policymakers.** . . . . . ($4)
IX. Bernard Rosen & Arthur C. Caplan, **Ethics in the Undergraduate Curriculum.** . . . . ($4)

TOTAL COST _____

PRICES QUOTED ARE POSTPAID—
PREPAYMENT IS REQUIRED
There will be a $1 service charge
if billing is necessary.

Name _____

Address _____

City _____ State _____ Zip Code _____